FOUNDATIONS OF MODERN HISTORY

General Editor A. Goodwin

Emeritus Professor of Modern History, University of Manchester

Origins of the First World War

by L. C. F. TURNER

Professor of History, Royal Military College of Australia

W · W · NORTON & COMPANY

New York · London

W. W. Norton & Company, Inc., 500 Fifth Avenue, New York, N.Y. 10110

COPYRIGHT © 1970 BY L. C. F. TURNER

ISBN 393-09947-4

Library of Congress Catalog Card No. 78-110514

PRINTED IN THE UNITED STATES OF AMERICA

6 7 8 9 0

General Preface

Historical controversy on the origins of the First World War has in the last decade taken on fresh dimensions since the publication of Fritz Fischer's *Griff nach der Weltmacht*.[1] In consequence, the diplomatic aspects of the international crisis of 1914, which had received such magisterial treatment at the hands of the Italian historian Albertini, have been viewed more recently in a wider political and economic context and Fischer's critics have also stressed the importance of the technical, military and strategical factors which influenced the thought and actions of the General Staffs both in their long-range defence preparations and in the final moves that precipitated armed conflict. Professor Turner's analysis of the complex issues which led to the coming of war in 1914 in the present volume is particularly useful as an introduction to such recent tendencies in the reinterpretation of the relative significance of these problems. In general, using additional evidence that has only recently become available to scholars, and critical of the more extreme views of the Fischer school, the author depicts the outbreak of the First World War as a 'tragedy of miscalculation'. He has drawn attention to the strength of pacific feeling in 1914 in the major European countries and to persistent misconceptions by historians about the attitudes and abilities of statesmen such as Bethmann Hollweg, Berchtold and Sazonov. His main contention is, however, that on the eve of hostilities few, if any, of the statesmen, whose saner judgment might have prevented the outbreak of war, had a serious understanding of the technical issues connected with mobilization and so they failed to grasp its strategical and political implications. As a result their decisions during the July crisis had unforeseen consequences and events slipped out of their control.

Above all what Professor Turner here provides is a succinct and critical account of the way in which the breakdown of international relations was finally precipitated in 1914 by the succession of diplomatic crises in the Mediterranean since 1905, by the intractable problem of Slav nationalism in the Balkans, the shifting balance of military advantage between the Central and

[1] English translation. *Germany's Aims in the First World War* (Norton paperback 1967). First German edition (Düsseldorf, 1961).

Entente powers and also, and not least, by the unexpected consequences of the strategical planning, armed preparations and final mobilization moves of the respective Defence Ministries and General Staffs. He has clearly demonstrated that no informed judgment on the real origins of the war in 1914 can be made without a proper understanding of Anglo-German naval competition, the successive modifications of the Schlieffen plan, the implications of the rival Austrian plans for mobilization against Russia and Serbia, the German assessment of the military threat of the French *réveil national*, and the dangers confronting the Central Powers as a result of the massive increase in the armed strength of Russia between 1912 and 1914.

A. GOODWIN

Abbreviations

The following abbreviations are used in the footnotes:

AJPH	*The Australian Journal of Politics and History*
*DD**	*Die deutschen Dokumente zum Kriegsausbruch 1914*, ed. W. Schücking and M. Monteglas. 4 vols. (Berlin, 1927)
*DDF**	*Documents Diplomatiques Français, 1871–1914.* 1st series 1871–1900; 2nd series 1901–1911; 3rd series 1911–1914 (Paris, 1929–40)
*GP**	*Die grosse Politik der europäischen Kabinette, 1871–1914.* 39 vols. (Berlin, 1922–7)
HJ	*The Historical Journal*
HZ	*Historische Zeitschrift*
JCH	*Journal of Contemporary History*
PP	*Past and Present*

After the initial reference, the following books are referred to only by the author's name:

L. Albertini	*The Origins of the War of 1914*, 3 vols. (London, 1965)
G. P. Gooch	*Recent Revelations of European Diplomacy* (London, 1940)
E. C. Helmreich	*The Diplomacy of the Balkan Wars, 1912–1913* (Cambridge, Mass., 1938)
A. J. P. Taylor.	*The Struggle for Mastery in Europe, 1848–1918* (Oxford, 1957)

* References to documents have been restricted to unusual items of exceptional importance.

Contents

Maps

The First Balkan War, 1912

Central Europe, 1914

Introduction

1910 was a year of relative calm in Europe. After a phase of tension and recurring crises between 1905 and 1909, the year marked an interlude when peace and co-operation among the Great Powers seemed to be a practicable objective. However, in 1911 the political climate changed and bitter diplomatic exchanges, combined with a great acceleration in the armaments race, led Europe remorselessly towards the catastrophe of 1914.

The roots of the great conflict can be traced far back into the nineteenth century, although it is unusual to begin the story of war origins earlier than 1871. The Congress of Berlin, the forming of the great alliances and the deepening shadow which spread over Anglo-German relations after the fall of Bismarck are vital elements in the background of the war. This short study does not attempt to evaluate these questions and concentrates on the period 1911–14 when statesmen perceptibly lost grip of their ability to direct events.

The situation in 1910 presented grave problems but was not beyond control. A. J. P. Taylor has remarked that 'no war is inevitable until it breaks out' and, even if this comment is of dubious validity for 1914, it certainly applies to the period between the end of the Bosnian crisis in March 1909 and the despatch of the gunboat *Panther* to Agadir in July 1911. Although there had been a serious deterioration in international relations since 1905, it would be difficult to argue that the first Moroccan and Bosnian crises had fatally prejudiced the maintenance of European peace. Nevertheless these ominous tests of strength had revealed very disquieting tendencies in German policy.

Modern German historians have stressed the 'will to power' in Imperial Germany, and close study of the trends between 1890 and 1909 does much to confirm the views which Fritz Fischer and Imanuel Geiss have presented in their provocative and interesting writings. German relations with Britain worsened sharply after the Kruger telegram of 1896, while the strict neutrality which the Kaiser and his ministers maintained during the South African War could not disguise the impression that 'the German people had displayed throughout the whole of that period, more animosity, envy and hatred of England than the people of any other country.'[1] Germany's commercial expansion, the giant growth of her coal and steel industries, the development of her dockyards and overseas shipping, and the doctrine of *Weltpolitik* openly proclaimed by many of her industrial and academic leaders received sharper emphasis with the building of a High Seas Fleet.

Fischer pictures the Germany Navy Laws of 1898 and 1900 as an inevitable product of German economic expansion and 'straining after world power'.[2] Whatever the truth of this view – and it seems to underestimate the great personal role of the Kaiser in building up the German Navy – it is indisputable that the activities of the Navy League backed by heavy industry were hardly calculated to enhance Germany's image in Britain. The law of 1900 openly proclaimed Alfred von Tirpitz's risk theory: 'In order to protect German trade and commerce under existing conditions, only one thing will suffice, namely, Germany must possess a battle fleet of such a strength that even for the most powerful naval adversary, a war would involve such risks as to make that Power's own supremacy doubtful.'

Yet it is easy to exaggerate the factors making for Anglo-German hostility in the early twentieth century. By 1905 the German Navy was a factor in the European balance, but the British superiority was still overwhelming and was likely to remain so for a long period. Taylor says:

> Liberal opinion looked with admiration at German industry and local government; Chamberlain was by no means the only radical who thought that Great Britain had more in common with Germany than with any other European Power. The trade rivalry which had made some stir ten years before was now less acute; Great Britain was entering on a new period of prosperity, much of which depended on German custom.[3]

A policy of restraint and caution offered much for Germany in 1905; it might well have led to an Anglo-German *rapprochement* and a dissolution of the Anglo-French entente signed in April 1904. But Bernhard von Bülow, the Chancellor, and Friedrich von

[1] Count Metternich, the German ambassador in London, summarizing British newspaper opinion. B. von Bülow, *Memoirs 1903–1909* (London, 1931), p. 2.

[2] F. Fischer, *Germany's Aims in the First World War* (London, 1967), p. 17.

[3] A. J. P. Taylor, *The Struggle for Mastery in Europe 1848–1918* (Oxford, 1957), p. 425.

Holstein, his principal adviser, had completely misjudged the character of the entente and did not perceive that its essential purpose was to preserve Britain and France from involvement in the Russo-Japanese War. By sending the Kaiser to Tangier on 31 March 1905 in an endeavour to shatter what they regarded as an incipient Anglo-French alliance, they precipitated a major international crisis.

The Tangier incident occurred at a time when the pattern of world politics was still relatively fluid. As Taylor remarks, the Dogger Bank episode of October 1904 marked the end of an epoch 'in which an Anglo-Russian conflict seemed the most likely outcome of international relations'. The Russo-Japanese War had relieved Britain's anxieties regarding her position in India and China, while by March 1905 the Anglo-French entente 'formed primarily to prevent a general war arising out of the Far East, had lost its main *raison d'être*'.[4] The Triple Alliance had been weakened by Italy's secret neutrality agreement with France in 1902, but the Franco-Russian alliance was far from being a rigid combination and Russo-German negotiations had made considerable headway in 1904.

By threatening war over Morocco, Germany drove Britain and France together, and the sanctioning of military conversations between the British and French General Staffs by the new Liberal Government in January 1906 gave the entente some of the characteristics of an alliance. Russia remained faithful to her ties with France – largely because of her desperate need of loans on the Paris market – while on taking office Sir Edward Grey, the Foreign Secretary, informed his ambassador in Paris that 'if France is let in for a war with Germany arising out of our agreement with her about Morocco we cannot stand aside, but must take part with France.'

There has been much speculation about Germany's motives in the Moroccan crisis and scholars of high standing have contended that war with France was the ultimate aim of German policy. Fischer declares that 'at least Holstein, the most influential member of the Foreign Ministry, and [Alfred von] Schlieffen, Chief of the General Staff from 1892 to 1906, were ready, if necessary, to detach France from the entente by force.' Gordon Craig says that Schlieffen 'felt that Germany's power position was slowly

[4] G. Monger, *The End of Isolation, British Foreign Policy 1900–1907* (London, 1963), p. 184.

being altered for the worse, and he would have welcomed an opportunity to stop its decline by a victorious war against France.' He adds that 'Holstein shared Schlieffen's fears for the future and would also have welcomed a trial by arms.'[5] These views are unsupported by serious documentary evidence and have been sharply challenged by Gerhard Ritter. He does not dispute that Schlieffen was impressed by the dismal showing of the Russian Army against Japan, and admits that he may have indulged in bellicose talk. However, Ritter emphasizes that 'there is no reliable documentary evidence for the statement that Graf Schlieffen urged the Kaiser or Bülow to make war against France during the Moroccan crisis.'[6] Ritter is even more emphatic that Holstein was not in favour of pushing the Moroccan crisis to the point of war. His view is fully confirmed by the relevant volume of *The Holstein Papers*, published in 1963, which contains no document indicating a desire on Holstein's part for preventive war.

At the Algeciras Conference in January–March 1906 German hopes of securing the support of Russia, Italy and the United States proved completely unfounded. In the final agreement, signed on 7 April, France gained the right to re-organize Moroccan finances and control the Moroccan police, with Spain as a junior partner. Germany had to be content with assurances about the 'open door' and free trade in Morocco on a basis of equality for all nations. Norman Rich thus summarizes the crisis:

At no stage of the Moroccan affair was a military solution ever advocated or seriously contemplated by the German leaders primarily responsible for Germany's Moroccan policy. On the contrary, the Kaiser, Bülow and also Holstein went to extreme lengths to avoid war; they allowed themselves to be miserably duped and in the end they submitted

[5] G. A. Craig, *Europe since 1815* (New York, 1966), p. 480.

[6] G. Ritter, *The Schlieffen Plan* (New York, 1958), pp. 111–12. See also L. C. F. Turner, 'The Significance of the Schlieffen Plan'. *AJPH* April 1967.

In *Weltmacht oder Niedergang* (Frankfurt, 1965), p. 40 Fischer reiterates his view that Schlieffen and Holstein pressed the Kaiser to go to war in 1905. He actually attaches importance to the comment in the Kaiser's letter of 31 December 1905: 'Shoot down the Socialists first, behead them, put them out of action, if necessary per blood bath – and then war abroad! But not before, and not *a tempo!*' Bülow says of this rhodomontade: 'The Kaiser's fear of war was expressed in every line of this letter.' Bülow, *Memoirs 1903–1909*, p. 191.

In *The Politics of the Prussian Army 1640–1945* (Oxford, 1955), p. 286, Gordon Craig says that Schlieffen was dismissed in January 1906 'for his advocacy of preventive war in 1905'. Ritter, *The Schlieffen Plan* pp. 109–11 has shown that this assertion is quite unfounded.

to a humiliating diplomatic defeat while their army was still capable of dictating the destinies of the states of Europe. Neither the Kaiser's nor Holstein's was a war policy, it was merely a stupid policy . . .[7]

The conclusion of the Anglo-Russian entente in August 1907 can be regarded as a natural reaction by Grey to German threats during the Moroccan crisis. George Monger says that 'Grey's own statements leave no doubt that his chief motive in seeking a Russian entente was to change the balance of forces in Europe and in particular to create a counterpoise to Germany.' The British move towards Russia sharpened the Anglo-German antagonism created by the accelerating naval race and the competition in dreadnought construction which developed from 1906 onwards. By 1908 the German fear of 'encirclement' was genuine enough. Fischer is justified in his contention that German policy since 1896 was largely responsible for this situation, but miscalculations rather than any conscious bid for 'world power' had forced what Fischer calls 'an iron ring around Germany'.[8] In Rich's words, the building up of the German Fleet 'had become a positive mania with the Kaiser', and in addition the formidable personality of Tirpitz, the chauvinism of the Navy League, and the dependence of the German steel industry on regular naval contracts had added an almost irresistible momentum to the 'Big Navy' programme. Britain reacted in 1909 by deciding to lay down eight dreadnought battleships in a single financial year.

The Bosnian crisis of 1908–9 exploded against this background

---

[7] N. Rich, *Friedrich von Holstein* (Cambridge, 1965), II, p. 745.

It is extremely doubtful whether the German Army in 1905 was capable of 'dictating the destinies of the states of Europe'. France conscripted a much higher proportion of her manpower than Germany and, if the French Army had fought on the defensive, a German assault would probably have been halted with heavy casualties within a measurable distance of the French frontier. The effect of the Dreyfus case on the morale and efficiency of the French Army has been much exaggerated. The French General Staff had not yet succumbed to the attractions of the Napoleonic Legend and had yet to evolve the fantastic Plan XVII which led to disaster in the Battle of the Frontiers in 1914.

[8] In his famous memorandum of 1 January 1907 Eyre Crowe, a high official at the British Foreign Office, emphasized Germany's desire to become a 'World Power' and remarked that Britain's tradition of hostility to any nation aspiring to such a role 'assumes almost the form of a law of nature'. However, Crowe did not see in German actions any deliberate plan of expansion and conquest; rather he envisaged German policy as 'the expression of a vague, confused and unpractical statesmanship, not fully realizing its own drift.'

of naval tension and deteriorating relations between Germany and Britain. For some years there had been indications that both the Ottoman and Austro-Hungarian empires faced a deadly threat from the resurgent nationalism of the Balkan peoples. The ruthless racial policy of the Hungarians had aroused bitter feelings among Croats and Serbs in the Dual Monarchy and contributed to the idea of a Great Yugoslavia. Since 1903 relations between the Habsburg Monarchy and the Kingdom of Serbia had been deteriorating. The murder of King Alexander and his Queen Draga in 1903 removed the Obrenovich dynasty, generally favourable to Austria, and led to Alexander's replacement by Peter Karageorgevich, whose family was traditionally attached to Russia. Under his rule parliamentary and democratic institutions developed in Serbia and the Radical Party under Nicholas Pasich attempted to break the country's economic dependence on Austria. A Serbo-Bulgarian customs agreement in 1905 met with severe retaliation by Austria, who closed her market to Serbian livestock. Serbia emerged victorious from the resulting 'Pig War', and found alternative markets in the Balkans, Egypt and Germany. France replaced Austria as the principal lender to Serbia; French credits provided Serbia with armaments and stimulated her commerce and industry.

Serbia was potentially the most explosive element in the Balkans. She had made a remarkable recovery from her defeat by Bulgaria in 1885 and was looking covetously towards the Serb lands of Bosnia and Montenegro, the Austro-Hungarian territories of Dalmatia, Slavonia and Croatia, and the storm-wracked Turkish *villayets* on her southern border. After 1903 Russian influence increased in Belgrade, and Serbian patriotic clubs founded branches in Bosnia and Hungary. The Serbs looked back to the fourteenth-century empire of Stephen Dushan, while Austrian ministers, only too conscious of the danger they faced from national minorities, were referring to Serbia as 'the Piedmont of the South Slavs'.

In its initial phases the Bosnian crisis had nothing to do with Germany; and even Fischer and Geiss have not ventured to maintain that the crisis was caused by *Weltpolitik*. Complicated negotiatiations between the Russian Foreign Minister, Alexander Izvolski, and his Austrian counterpart, Alois von Aehrenthal, reached a climax in their meeting at Count Berchtold's Castle of Buchlau in Moravia on 16 September 1908. Izvolski wanted

Austrian support for a revision of the Treaty of Berlin by re-opening the Bosphorus and Dardanelles to Russian warships. Aehrenthal had rejected the advice of the Austrian Chief of Staff, Conrad von Hötzendorf, who had been pressing for a preventive war against Serbia since 1906 and demanding the extermination of that 'dangerous nest of vipers'; he had also renounced his own plan for curbing Serbia by constructing a railway line through the Sanjak of Novibazar, a Turkish district under Austrian military control and strategically important because it separated Serbia from Montenegro. Aehrenthal now wanted to check Serbian nationalism by formally annexing the Turkish provinces of Bosnia and Herzegovina, which Austria had been administering since they were entrusted to her by the Congress of Berlin of 1878.

The situation demanded swift action by Austria because it seemed that the 'Young Turks', installed in power at Constantinople by the revolution of July 1908, intended to confer parliamentary representation on the occupied provinces. Aehrenthal's motives are clear enough, but Izvolski had completely failed to prepare Russian public opinion and, although he had obtained the Tsar's consent to the negotiations, had refrained from consulting the Prime Minister, Stolypin. Izvolski afterwards complained that he had been grossly deceived by Aehrenthal, but he had only himself to blame for raising a question of no urgency to Russia and for consenting in his note of 2 July – in complete disregard of Slav sentiment – to Austria's annexation of Bosnia, Herzegovina and even the Sanjak of Novibazar. He certainly anticipated that these matters would be referred to a European conference, but Aehrenthal had the annexation of Bosnia and Herzegovina proclaimed on 6 October 1908, while on the previous day Ferdinand of Bulgaria renounced Turkish suzerainty and assumed the title of 'Tsar'.

These developments came as a bombshell, not only to the entente powers but also to Germany and Turkey. The Kaiser denounced Aehrenthal's action as 'a subaltern's rag', while in Russia and Serbia the public indignation was intense. Izvolski learned of the annexation in Paris, where he discovered that the French Government of Clemenceau was far from enthusiastic about a re-opening of the Straits. In London he received cold comfort from Grey, who coupled approval of Russian naval access to the Mediterranean, with a request for a right of entry by foreign warships into the Black Sea. As Taylor says, 'No proposal could have been more repugnant to Russia.' Izvolski took refuge in abuse of Aehrenthal and loudly demanded the summoning of a European conference.

Serbia believed herself menaced by Austrian invasion and instituted a partial mobilization. Her demands for 'compensation' were coupled with the founding of the *Narodna Obrana* (National Defence) society to further her interests in the lost provinces. Austria reinforced her troops in Bosnia, and eventually Conrad was given authority to ask Helmuth von Moltke, the German Chief of Staff, what support he would provide in the event of an Austro-Russian war. With the approval of the Kaiser and Bülow, Moltke replied on 21 January 1909 that, 'the moment Russia mobilizes, Germany will also mobilize, and will unquestionably mobilize her whole army.' For the first time the conception of the Schlieffen Plan was disclosed to Austria, and Conrad was informed of Moltke's intention to hurl the main body of the German forces first against France. Moltke said: 'It is to be foreseen that the time will come when the longanimity of the Monarchy in face of Serb provocation will come to an end. Then nothing will remain but for her to enter Serbia.'

Russian intervention was considered improbable, but it seems that Bülow and Moltke were anxious to take advantage of her weakness and settle the Serbian question once and for all. This appears to be the reason for Germany's intervention in St. Petersburg on 22 March 1909, insisting that Russia should recognize the annexation of Bosnia and bring pressure on Serbia to do likewise. This veiled ultimatum contains the ominous words: '. . . we expect a definite answer: Yes or No; any evasive, involved, or vague answer would have to be regarded by us as a refusal. We would then withdraw and let matters take their course.'

The Russian Government was firmly resolved to avoid war at any cost and yielded immediately to Bülow's demand. The documentary evidence is not conclusive, but the Chancellor's objective seems to have been to let Austria loose against Serbia and frighten Russia with a display of the 'mailed fist'. On 27 March a Council of Ministers in Vienna, presided over by Aehrenthal and attended by Conrad, actually decided on mobilization against Serbia but the decision was reversed on the following day. Aehrenthal decided to be content with a dramatic diplomatic success, and on 2 April Conrad voiced his bitter indignation in a letter to Franz Josef. He emphasized that the solution of the annexation crisis was but an illusory triumph for the Monarchy, and deplored the failure to crush Serbia and Montenegro. He declared: 'These two foes have neither been beaten nor crushed by diplomatic procedure but have been roused and made aware of their weakness. They will certainly not fail to take the lesson to heart.' Conrad warned the Emperor that, as a result of her forbearance, Austria would one day find herself involved in a war on several fronts.

One of the most important by-products of the Bosnian crisis was Aehrenthal's decision in October 1908 to withdraw Austrian troops from the Sanjak of Novibazar. He hoped thereby to conciliate the Turks, but his action was to have disastrous consequences for Austria on the outbreak of the Balkan Wars.

CHAPTER ONE

Morocco and the Powers, 1909–1912

GERMAN policy in March 1909 has been severely criticized but, if Austria had taken advantage of the opening made for her by Bülow, Serbia would have been crushed and Russian influence in the Balkans might have been eliminated indefinitely. Bülow and the acting Foreign Secretary, Kiderlen-Wächter, had carried out a ruthless stroke of power politics in the Bismarckian tradition, but Austria's refusal to strike nullified Bülow's attempt 'to tear the encirclement net to pieces'. This short-term diplomatic success was offset by the bitter hostility of Russia and Serbia and the deep suspicions which Austro-German policy had aroused in London and Paris. The Bosnian affair foreshadowed the greater crisis of July 1914 and contributed notably to that *dénouement*.

Bülow was far from being the vulgar trifler pictured by many British historians. A man of wide culture and brilliant oratorical powers, he had no desire to plunge Germany into a struggle for world domination. To some extent he had been dragged along by the Kaiser's naval policy and indeed could hardly have retained office without giving it substantial support. By April 1909 he was alarmed at the furious denunciations which the policy was arousing in Britain and warned Tirpitz that, 'England will oppose us in the whole world and . . . take the first opportunity, together with the other European powers, to attack us.' In Bülow's view, 'this could be in two years, as soon as the reorganization of the Russian Army is completed.' In conversations with the Kaiser and Admiral von Müller, Chief of his Naval Cabinet on 14/15 April, Bülow 'expressed again and again great apprehension about the maintenance of peace.' But Tirpitz remained unshaken in his stubborn conviction that economic jealousy rather than naval rivalry was the root cause of British hostility. The Grand-Admiral declared that Germany was 'exposed to economic impoverishment through the ruthless behaviour of the English', and insisted that there must be no slackening of the naval programme. Nor would he listen to suggestions by Admiral Galster that Germany's defensive needs would be better served by light cruisers, submarines and coast defences than by battleships.

Bülow left office in July 1909; and his successor, Theobald von Bethmann Hollweg, was left to grapple with the intractable Tirpitz and the perennial naval problem. Descendant of a famous Frankfurt banking family, Bethmann had risen steadily in the Prussian Civil Service and in 1909 was Reich Secretary of the Interior. He had displayed considerable abilities in law and administration and gained a high reputation for personal integrity. To Lord Haldane he gave the impression of 'an honest man struggling somewhat with adversity'. He was certainly anxious to achieve good relations with Britain, but viewed Russian aims and policy with deep suspicion. A sombre and uninspiring personality, he knew little of foreign affairs and tended to view the course of events with what the Crown Prince has described as 'a passive fatalism.'

Such a man was hardly likely to cope with the masterful Tirpitz, supported by the Kaiser and the very powerful political and industrial groups which backed the German naval programme. Nevertheless, between August 1909 and June 1911, Bethmann attempted to secure a British assurance of neutrality in a continental war in return for a slowing down of the tempo of German naval construction. A. J. Marder says that 'it is noteworthy that Grey never revealed to the British people that the Germans were ready to discuss naval limitation in return for a suitable political agreement.'[1] Actually both governments were anxious to avoid publicity. Grey knew how much the Radicals wanted to reduce expenditure on armaments while, in Marder's words, Bethmann had to reckon with 'the ire of the German Navy League, Anglophobes, imperialists etc.'

The Press of both countries continued to work up public emotions. In December 1909 the *Daily Mail* published a series of articles on 'England and Germany', which declared that Germany was aiming at 'world dominion' and 'cold-bloodedly' preparing to destroy the British Empire. Nor were such views confined to the popular newspapers. In 1910 Sir Arthur Nicolson, former ambassador in St. Petersburg, took over as Under-Secretary at the Foreign Office; Lady Wemyss relates that at

[1] A. J. Marder, *From the Dreadnought to Scapa Flow*, Vol. I (London, 1961), p. 232.

a dinner party in June 1911 he reacted violently to suggestions for an Anglo-German *rapprochement* and 'jumping up as if he had been stung . . . emphatically declared that as long as *he* was at the head of the Foreign Office, England should never, never be friends with Germany'.[2]

Balked of an understanding with Britain, Bethmann was more willing to listen to approaches from Russia. In November 1910 the Tsar and Sazonov, his new Foreign Minister, visited Potsdam and offered to drop Russia's long-standing opposition to the Bagdad railway, if Germany would respect Russia's special interests in northern Persia. The Russian offer was probably a manoeuvre to bring pressure on Britain, where there was strong criticism of Russia's crushing of the Persian liberals and support of the reactionary Shah. No formal agreement was concluded at Potsdam, but the Russian move aroused much anxiety in London and Paris.

Taylor goes so far as to say that, 'the Triple Entente seemed in process of disintegration', and considers that it was saved by German policy in Morocco. It is certainly true that in the winter of 1910–11, as in the first months of 1905, Germany had a choice between a policy of cautious circumspection, designed to divide her potential enemies, and some bold and spectacular stroke. The new Foreign Secretary, Kiderlen-Wächter, chose the latter alternative.

Kiderlen was a singular character. Having incurred the wrath of the Kaiser, he had spent many years as German minister in Bucharest. During the Bosnian crisis, he had been summoned to Berlin where he gave an impression of being ruthless and inclined to bluster and swagger. Lord Haldane commented in 1912 that he 'would not trust him one inch', while Sazonov wrote in his memoirs:

It would be difficult to imagine a man of less attractive exterior. The more he endeavoured to display gentleness and amiability in his manner, the more his innate roughness revealed itself. . . . But for all that he was indisputably a man of ability, closely acquainted with all the details of the international situation.[3]

There was no adequate reason why 'the Swabian Bismarck', as

[2] W. Wemyss, *The Life and Letters of Lord Wester Wemyss* (London, 1935), pp. 127–8.

[3] S. Sazonov, *Fateful Years 1909–1916* (London, 1928), p. 29.

his admirers called him, should have chosen to force the issue in Morocco. Franco-German relations in recent years had been reasonably good. In 1908 a sharp dispute over the actions of the German consul in Casablanca in assisting deserters from the Foreign Legion had been resolved by arbitration; while in February 1909 the two powers signed an agreement on Morocco, which promised Germany full economic equality in that country. The French firm of Schneider-Creusot discussed with Krupps the exploitation of Moroccan mining interests; indeed so far from being bitter rivals French and German capitalists were happy to co-operate. (The most striking example is the infiltration of German finance into the French ironfields of Longwy-Briey.) There were in fact powerful elements in France, who favoured an understanding with Germany. Taylor says: 'Radicals of the Rouvier school aspired to a Franco-German financial partnership, in which Germany would run the risks of the ordinary shareholder and France would be the holder of secure debentures; Caillaux, Minister of Finance, now led this party.' The Socialist leader, Jean Jaurès, was on excellent terms with German Social Democrats; he longed to heal the wound of 1870 and would gladly have repudiated the Franco-Russian alliance. Jaurès denounced French loans to 'the most barbarous of tyrannies'.

Kiderlen was in some respects the prisoner of forces, which he had encouraged and could no longer control. The Pan-German League never had more than 34 representatives in the Reichstag, but its membership included prominent industrialists and professors and it was supported by a powerful Press. While colonialists were demanding the creation of a *Mittelafrika*, which would absorb the French and Belgian Congo and create an empire stretching from the Kamerun to Tanganyika, the Pan-Germans stressed Germany's mission to unite all the German-speaking peoples of Europe, including the Swiss and the Dutch, and assert her supremacy in South America and Africa. In 1909 Kiderlen remarked to Class, the Chairman of the Pan-German League:

I never understood why my predecessors were so hostile to you. It is useful for the Government in foreign relations to be able to appeal to the Pan-Germans. . . . Watch and if necessary criticize my policy. Then I can say that the Foreign Office is prepared for compromise, but that there are the wicked Pan-Germans whose influence is too great to be ignored.[4]

[4] G. P. Gooch, *Recent Revelations of European Diplomacy* (London, 1940), p. 82, quoting Class *Wider den Strom*.

In a sense Fischer is correct in contending that the Agadir crisis was caused by the conceptions of *Weltpolitik* and *Mittelafrika*. Yet the issues were exceedingly complicated, and it is futile to picture the crisis in the black and white terms favoured by anti-imperialists of the Hobson-Lenin school. Taylor argues that by 1911 the Germans were victims of their own propaganda and that 'a prolonged campaign by private interests had taught the German people that Morocco represented a great economic prize.' He denies that Morocco saw a clash between French and German steel-interests and says: 'Mannesmann Brothers, an interloping German firm, sought to break the Krupp–Thyssen monopoly by inventing shady claims in Morocco and posing as the defender of German national interests. Mannesmann worked with the Pan-Germans and organized agitation in the Reichstag . . .'[5]

In Paris also various cross-currents confused the situation. Shady financiers devised schemes for Franco-German co-operation in railway and rubber concessions in the Congo and Kamerun. Although Caillaux, who was appointed Minister of Finance in March 1911, favoured co-operation, he profoundly distrusted the financiers involved and vetoed the proposals. Meanwhile quarrels in Morocco between Mannesmann Brothers and the French *Union des Mines* sharpened Franco-German tension. The French were now in semi-permanent occupation of Casablanca; and chronic disorders in Morocco gave them an excuse for a steady extension of their police and military control. The Sultan was compelled by an ultimatum to accept a loan, which brought him more completely under French domination. Public executions of Moroccan deserters by Colonel Mangin underlined the realities of French occupation.

A swelling hostility towards Europeans culminated in a large-scale revolt in the Fez district. In March 1911 the Sultan appealed to France to protect his capital against the insurgent tribes, and on 5 April Jules Cambon, the French ambassador in Berlin, informed Kiderlen that it would be necessary to take military action. The Foreign Secretary received the announcement quietly but declared that a French occupation of Fez would fall outside the Algeciras agreement and should only be resorted to in extreme need. On 19 April Bethmann Hollweg advised France against the expedition on the ground that it would arouse German public

[5] Taylor, p. 465 *n.*

opinion and lead to a holy war in Morocco. On 23 April the French Cabinet of Monis decided to send a military force to occupy Fez, but it did not reach the Moroccan capital until 21 May. By that time Kiderlen had formulated his policy.

There is no doubt that both the Kaiser and Bethmann Hollweg were anxious to avoid trouble over Morocco.[6] Wilhelm thought that it would be to Germany's advantage if France squandered troops and treasure in Morocco which could be used to strengthen her Rhine frontier. Kiderlen, however, had different ideas, reflected in his conversation with Class, the Pan-German leader, on 19 April:

> It is a question whether we try for naval bases or for a colony, as you wish. The Admiralty is against naval bases, as they divide the fleet. Kiao-Chau is enough. Your plan of a colony is different, for the fate of colonies will be decided in Europe in the event of war. It will be useful to raise demands in the press and in meetings. Such a division of labour between the Foreign Office and the unions [i.e. leagues] is desirable. Then I can say, 'I am ready for compromise but public opinion must be considered'. We shall stand firm in Morocco though we may seem to draw back a step. . . . You may be sure that our Morocco policy will please you. You will be satisfied.[7]

On 3 May Kiderlen formulated his policy in a lengthy memorandum to the Kaiser. He proposed to declare that a French occupation of Fez violated the Treaty of Algeciras and entitled Germany to compensations. As a pledge, he proposed to despatch warships to Agadir and Mogador on the pretext of protecting German lives. He did not anticipate trouble with Britain, and the Kaiser assented to this plan on 11 May.[8]

Kiderlen's forceful personality and devious diplomacy now combined to drag Germany into one of the most disastrous of her pre-war adventures. On 19 June the Managing Director of the Hamburg-Morocco Company was asked by the German Foreign Ministry to collect from interested firms a petition asking for official protection in Morocco. This was duly presented on 21 June; on the same day Kiderlen told Cambon that Germany 'must be compensated' and asked him to 'bring us back something from Paris.' Meanwhile Caillaux was promising Kiderlen in

[6] *GP* XXIX, Nos. 10538, 10539, 10542.
[7] Gooch, p. 83.
[8] *GP* XXIX, No. 10549. See also Joanne S. Mortimer, 'Commercial Interests and German Diplomacy in the Agadir Crisis', *HJ*, No. 3, 1967.

unofficial negotiations that Germany would receive a generous *quid pro quo*. On 23 June an air accident necessitated changes in the French Government, and on 28 June Caillaux became Prime Minister. Germany had only to wait for a very satisfactory French offer to fall into her lap. But on 26 June Kiderlen and Bethmann Hollweg had seen the Kaiser at Kiel, and induced him to consent to divert the gunboat *Panther* to Agadir, ostensibly to protect German interests, although there was not a German within seventy miles. In Kiderlen's view, Germany would get no serious concessions unless she 'threw her weight about'.

On 1 July Zimmermann, Under-Secretary at the Foreign Ministry, announced proudly to Class:

> In a quarter of an hour the bomb explodes. At twelve our ambassadors announce the arrival of the *Panther* at Agadir. We have caused German firms and business men to send complaints and appeals. We chose Agadir because no French or Spaniards are there. It leads to the Sus, the richest mineral and agricultural part of South Morocco. . . . We shall take and keep this district as we need a place to settle in.

The official announcement of the *Panther's* 'spring' had the same effect as the Kaiser's Tangier speech of March 1905 and, in Churchill's words 'all the alarm bells throughout Europe began immediately to quiver.' Although the French Press was at first not particularly disturbed, the French Government took the move very seriously and there were signs of acute anxiety in Britain. In the Foreign Office, Sir Arthur Nicolson assumed that the Germans intended to acquire a port on the Moroccan coast and turn it into a second Heligoland. Grey was so concerned that his first reaction was to acquiesce in a French request to send a British warship to Agadir, but the Cabinet overruled him on 4 July. In fact the Admiralty indicated that it had no serious objection to a German base on the Atlantic coast of Morocco; the British Naval Staff, like the German, appreciated that such a base would merely divide and weaken the German Fleet. It is significant that Tirpitz was not consulted about the despatch of the *Panther*.

In Germany the more intelligent members of the business world were not particularly impressed by Kiderlen's forceful diplomacy and Albert Ballin, General Director of the Hamburg-America Company, asked why Germany 'should send a ship to Agadir and excite the whole world to white heat?' On the other hand the Pan-German and nationalist newspapers were 'deliriously enthusiastic'. The *Rheinisch-Westfälische Zeitung* commented on 2 July that, if France did not yield 'then may the *Panther* have the effect of the Ems Despatch'.[9] Threats of war were not lacking in other papers, and only the Social Democrat Press roundly condemned the move.

In his own terminology, Kiderlen now proceeded to 'thump the table'; in conversation with Jules Cambon on 15 July he had the effrontery to demand the whole of the French Congo, in return for waiving Germany's claims in Morocco, and indicated his readiness to 'proceed very forcibly'. These tactics alarmed the Kaiser, then on his Norwegian cruise, and Kiderlen was warned by a member of the imperial entourage that 'it will be very difficult to get His Majesty's consent to any measures he considers likely to lead to war.' Kiderlen was provoked into attempting resignation, when the Kaiser made it clear that he would not tolerate mobilization or further threats against France. The position of the Foreign Secretary was most unenviable for France was now in no mood to yield; anxious as Caillaux was to make concessions, he had to consider French public opinion and warlike ministers such as Delcassé, the Minister of Marine. On 18 July France informed Grey of Germany's exorbitant demands.

The upshot was the decision of the British Cabinet to issue a warning to Germany in Lloyd George's Mansion House speech of 21 July. The Chancellor of the Exchequer stressed that he would make great sacrifices to secure peace, but that to surrender vital British interests would be 'a humiliation intolerable for a great country like ours to endure'. It may be, as Taylor argues, that the statement that Britain was not to be held 'of no account in the cabinet of nations', was directed at Caillaux, but to the Germans it seemed either an insult or a veiled threat of war. Curiously enough the German newspapers did not react to the speech itself, but were jerked into action by British editorial comments upon it. There followed an explosion of wrath, which affected even the pacific Kaiser, and led to the statement by Count Metternich to Grey on 25 July that Germany would have to insist on observance of the Algeciras treaty, 'even by force of arms'.

[9] This and subsequent quotations from German newspapers have been taken from E. M. Carroll. *Germany and the Great Powers 1866–1914* (New York, 1938).

On 27 July the Prime Minister, Asquith, eased the tension in a fairly conciliatory speech, which indicated that Britain was not opposed to French concessions to Germany in West Africa. In the meantime, however, Britain was taking extensive naval precautions, while on 20 July General Wilson, the Director of Military Operations, discussed with the French General Staff the details of moving a British expeditionary force to France. The Admiralty did not awake to the perils of the situation until 25 July, when Grey told Winston Churchill and Lloyd George: 'I have just received a communication from the German ambassador so stiff that the Fleet might be attacked at any moment. I have sent for McKenna [First Lord of the Admiralty] to warn him.' In Marder's words, the Cabinet was 'shocked and amazed' to find that, in the absence from London of the First Sea Lord, the Admiralty could produce no war plan for the Navy. Indeed from the British point of view, Agadir did have certain beneficial consequences. The move of Churchill to the Admiralty in November 1911, was followed by a general 'shake-up', and by effective steps to remedy the extraordinary lack of harmony between War Office and Admiralty strategy. Plans for seizing islands in the Elbe estuary or breaking into the Baltic were put aside, and efforts were concentrated on covering the despatch of a British army to northern France.

Britain was the only power to take defensive measures in 1911, and prepare her fleet for action. With the approval of Messimy, the forceful but realistic French Minister of War, Caillaux was seeking a pacific formula, while Kiderlen was held in check by the Kaiser and was learning the truth of Holstein's bitter comment, 'it is no pleasure to handle high politics under a ruler who, one is well aware, will never fight.' When Jules Cambon called on Kiderlen on 2 August and offered him '*un gros morceau*' of the inner Congo, the Foreign Secretary was prepared to accept this as a basis for negotiation. A communiqué on 4 August indicated that Germany would be satisfied with less than the whole Congo; from that point the protracted negotiations masked a slow but perceptible German retreat.

While the temperament of the Kaiser and the inferiority of the German Navy were decisive for the preservation of peace, other factors contributed to a compromise solution. Austria had no interest in German ambitions in Morocco, while from St. Petersburg the French ambassador reported that 'Russian public opinion would hardly understand a war occasioned by a colonial question like Morocco.' On 1 September Izvolski, now ambassador in Paris, lectured de Selves, the French Foreign Minister, on Russia's wish for peace and the urgent need to strengthen her armaments. French and German socialists proclaimed their mutual solidarity in the fight for peace. The French withdrawal of short-term loans from the Berlin market, led to heavy falls on the stock exchange and demands from German financiers for a lessening of tension. Caillaux took over the conduct of negotiations from the incompetent de Selves and, in the final agreement signed on 4 November, Germany declared her readiness to recognize a French protectorate in Morocco, in return for substantial cessions of territory to give her colony of Kamerun access to the River Congo.

Outwardly all had ended well, but it is difficult to overestimate the importance of Agadir in the chain of events leading up to July 1914. The ramifications of the crisis were profound and will now be considered at length.

The first and most obvious consequence was Italy's decision to assert her right to 'compensation', promised in the Franco-Italian agreement of 16 December 1900, which laid down that Italy could occupy Tripolitania and Cyrenaica if France extended her influence in Morocco. The Triple Alliance had conceded Italy's right to take such action, in the various renewal agreements since 1887. The Russo-Italian secret agreement at Racconigi in October 1909 had agreed on common action to preserve the status quo in the Balkans, and had recognized Italian interests on the Libyan shore. On the night 26/27 September 1911 the Italian ambassador delivered an ultimatum in Constantinople demanding consent to an Italian occupation of Tripolitania and Cyrenaica within twenty-four hours. On 29 September Italy and Turkey were formally at war, and on 3 October an Italian squadron bombarded the fortress of Tripoli.

During October Italian troops were landed at various Libyan harbours, and the Italian expeditionary force was gradually built up to 100,000 men. Stubborn resistance by Turkish troops and Arab irregulars pinned the Italian garrisons close to the coast, with the result that Italy resorted to naval pressure. Attempts to enforce a blockade led to the stopping of French liners and sharp protests from France. More serious was the Italian seizure in May 1912 of the Dodecanese islands in the Aegean Sea, combined with bombardments and naval raids on the Dardanelles. This conflict seriously embarrassed Turkey and encouraged the Balkan states to attack her in 1912. With one of his occasional flashes of perception, the Kaiser remarked in October 1911 that Italy's action might be the first step towards 'a world war with all its terrors'.

In France the long-drawn Moroccan crisis deeply affected public opinion. In 1910 Barrès was bewailing that 'the idea of *revanche* was forgotten or dead' but E. Weber remarks that, 'The events of 1911 persuaded many of the pacific, the hesitant and the indifferent that the threat to France was real and that war was only a matter of time.'[10] The prevailing sentiment of the nation was reflected in the comment of *L'Aurore* on 6 September 1911:

France does not want war, but she would not refuse it at the cost of her honour. Her mind is made up. If war were to break out, it would be because we are attacked by an unscrupulous enemy who still believes that his force is sufficient excuse for all his brutalities.

Paul Deschanel remarked on 17 September 1911, 'the German fife has rallied France.' The first French reactions to the Morocco-Congo settlement of 4 November were favourable, but the publication of the Franco-Spanish agreement on 8 November caused disappointment. Many had hoped that France would gain the whole of Morocco and regretted the concessions made to Spain, while others argued that in any case colonies were of negligible value. The influential army journal, *La France Militaire*, declared in November 1911: 'Beside the lost provinces of Alsace and Lorraine, no colony, be it Tongking, Madagascar or Morocco is worth anything. "Alsace", "Lorraine", these two words cry out what the policy of France ought to be.'

Whatever the imperfections of the Moroccan settlement, there was a feeling that France had measured swords with Germany and emerged with victory. The *réveil national* showed its strength in January 1912, when Caillaux's Government fell and was replaced by that of Raymond Poincaré. The distinguished lawyer from Lorraine was a man of outstanding personality and intellectual power, and Fay remarks that 'no one since Bismarck's day has equalled him in sheer ability.' Denis Brogan says: 'The alarmed politicians of the old school of power diplomacy saw in

[10] E. Weber, *The Nationalist Revival in France 1905–1914* (Berkeley, 1959), p. 11.

Caillaux a dangerous diplomatic gambler, who was willing to throw away acquired French assets, like the Russian alliance and the entente with Britain, for problematic deals with Germany...'[11] Henceforward French policy would be guided by a remarkable statesman, who combined a firm belief in the Franco-Russian alliance with a deep hostility towards Germany.

If the German Government eventually made concessions to France, this was hardly due to the pressure of public opinion. There had been loud demands for 'a strong policy' and declarations that 'war was preferable to surrender.' Moltke, the Chief of Staff, reflected the opinions of many of his countrymen, when he wrote to his wife on 19 August 1911: 'If we again slink out of this affair with our tail between our legs, if we cannot pull ourselves together to present demands which we are prepared to enforce by the sword, then I despair of the future of the German Reich.'[12] Yet too much importance should not be attached to such outbursts, echoed in the militant columns of the nationalist and Pan-German Press. It was difficult for the post-Bismarckian generation, steeped in the traditions of Frederick the Great, Blücher and Moltke, to accept the very real limitations to German power or to acquiesce in the hard fact that France, with the support of Britain and Russia, was no longer dwelling in the shadow of 1870. The Germans were in a dangerous mood in 1911, but this was due less to a craving for *Weltpolitik* than to a sense of injured pride and an uneasy feeling that the balance of power was swinging against them.

The resignation of the Colonial Secretary, Lindequist, on 3 November 1911 reflected the opinions of those who regarded the Moroccan agreement as far more advantageous to France than to Germany. Although the Catholic *Germania* declared that the settlement should be 'warmly welcomed', the general reaction was extremely unfavourable. Carroll says that to the nationalists it was 'a national shame and the last nail in the coffin of Germany's prestige'. The British ambassador noted that some of the more extreme opinions were influenced by the

[11] D. Brogan, *The Development of Modern France* (London, 1940), p. 444.
[12] Quoted by I. Geiss, *July 1914* (London, 1967), p. 40. Geiss distorts the significance of this statement by saying that Moltke 'deplored that the chance had been lost to seek a showdown with Britain'. Whatever Moltke's limitations as a strategist, he was certainly not ignorant of the 2:1 superiority enjoyed by the Royal Navy in 1911.

impending general elections, but Bethmann Hollweg's attempt
to justify the Government's policy was ill-received by the Reichstag. The Chancellor claimed that England not Germany had
retreated, and he appealed to Bismarck's authority against the
theory of preventive war. The *Berliner Tageblatt* of 9 November
commented on the Reichstag's reception of Bethmann's speech:
'The silence was like that of the grave . . . Not a hand moved, no
applause rang out.' In contrast the Conservative leader, Heyde-
brand, was loudly cheered and ostentatiously applauded by the
Crown Prince from the Visitors' Gallery, when he said of Lloyd
George's Mansion House speech:

Such incidents like a flash in the dark show the German people where
is the foe. The German people now knows, when it seeks foreign expansion and a place in the sun, such as is its right and destiny, where it has to
look for permission. We Germans are not accustomed to that and cannot
allow it and we shall know how to answer.

Perhaps even more ominous were the speeches by the so-called
moderates of the Catholic Centre. Erzberger described England
as a more determined foe of German expansion than France,
while Count Hertling, the future Chancellor, warned France not
to presume too much on 'Germany's love of peace'.

Tirpitz took advantage of the situation to press for a supplementary Navy Law, intended to achieve a 2:3 ratio in capital
ships with the Royal Navy but, when he unfolded his proposals
in September 1911, Bethmann Hollweg remarked 'you are
leading us to war.' This was also the opinion of Count Metternich,
the ambassador in London, who wrote on 10 January 1912:

A *Novelle* will drive England again to the side of France and there she
will stay. We can no longer hide from ourselves that the English entente
system and her hostile policy towards us rest primarily on the fear of our
growing strength at sea. A navy policy going beyond the Navy Law leads
in my opinion to war.[13]

Bethmann Hollweg clutched at the prospect of a naval agreement, which appeared to emerge from preliminary discussions
between Albert Ballin and the British magnate of German birth,
Sir Ernest Cassel. Anglo-Russian relations in Persia had deterio-
rated sharply in 1911, and this may have strengthened the hand
of the radicals when they pressed the British Cabinet to try and

[13] Gooch, p. 52.

achieve some *modus vivendi* with Germany. Sir Edward Grey could not be induced to go to Berlin – in fact apart from a brief visit to Paris in April 1914, he never set foot on the Continent in his whole period of office – but Lord Haldane, the Minister of War, was sent to Germany to explore the possibilities of an understanding. If Germany cancelled the *Novelle*, Britain would endeavour to aid German colonial expansion and guarantee her against aggression. Haldane arrived in Berlin on 7 February 1912, the day on which the Kaiser announced impending naval and military increases in his opening speech to the Reichstag. On 9 February Churchill responded with a fiery speech in Glasgow, delivered without Cabinet approval, in which he described the German Navy as a 'luxury'. This ill-chosen expression aroused great resentment in Germany.

In the circumstances, the negotiations had little prospect of success. The Kaiser was never rational where naval issues were concerned, while Tirpitz was utterly determined on the *Novelle*. The British move was watched with deep suspicion in Paris, while Grey was resolved to do nothing to prejudice the entente. Haldane was well received in Berlin but, on his return to London, all efforts to find a 'formula', which would satisfy both Germany and France proved unavailing. Asquith commented reasonably enough in a letter to Grey on 10 April:

I agree that the French are somewhat unduly nervous. But I confess I am becoming more and more doubtful as to the wisdom of prolonging these discussions with Germany about a formula. Nothing, I believe, will meet her purpose which falls short of a promise on our part of neutrality, a promise we cannot give. And she makes no firm or solid offer even in exchange for that.

There is no doubt that Bethmann Hollweg was desperately anxious to reach an agreement with Britain; he understood the folly of the *Novelle* and offered to resign. The Kaiser persuaded him to remain at his post, but the Chancellor began to crack under the strain. Marder says: 'On 18 March, after the arrival of Grey's amended formula, the Emperor found Bethmann Hollweg in a state of collapse and pressed a glass of port wine on him.'

The *Novelle* was admirably calculated to force Britain into a closer relationship with France. On 14 February 1912 Churchill reported to the Cabinet that 'the German Navy Law was much worse than they had thought.' In his view, its most serious feature was not so much the addition of three dreadnoughts, nor even the creation of a third battle squadron, 'but the extraordinary increase in the striking force of ships of all classes immediately available throughout the year.' Of 144 German destroyers, 99 were to be continuously manned and ready for action, while 72 U-boats were to be built, of which 54 would have full crews. In other words, Britain had to be ready for war at any moment; in May 1912 she organized a Home Fleet, with 33 battleships in full commission and 8 with skeleton crews, to cope with the 25 German battleships available without mobilization.[14] Churchill warned the House of Commons of the 'formidable character' of the German High Seas Fleet, 'designed for aggressive and offensive action of the largest possible character in the North Sea or the North Atlantic.' He pointed out that the striking power of this fleet would be greatly increased with the widening of the Kiel Canal in 1914.

In the summer of 1912, Britain withdrew most of her naval strength from the Mediterranean. Although four battle-cruisers were to be stationed at Malta, and a battle squadron would still be based at Gibraltar, the centre of gravity of British naval power was shifting northwards. The *Standard* wrote on 29 May: 'Because of that formidable and threatening Armada across the North Sea, we have almost abandoned the waters of the Outer Oceans.' In July Churchill had talks with the French naval attaché and in August the Cabinet approved formal naval conversations with France. In September the French Brest Fleet moved to Toulon, which meant that France would now assume the major naval responsibilities in the Mediterranean, where her concentrated fleet would counter-balance the navies of Austria and Italy. On 10 February 1913 Britain and France signed a technical agreement for naval co-operation in time of war.

Britain had now incurred a moral obligation to defend the French Channel and Atlantic coasts. It is true that the British Cabinet declined to admit that any such obligation existed, and that Grey told Paul Cambon, the French ambassador, in November 1912 that discussions between military and naval experts did not constitute 'an engagement that commits either government to action in a contingency that has not arisen and may never arise.' However, it was agreed that in the event of a

[14] These totals include pre-dreadnought battleships.

crisis both governments would immediately discuss measures 'to prevent aggression and to preserve peace'. As a result of Agadir and the *Novelle*, the Anglo-French entente was now virtually a military alliance.[15]

[15] According to Marder, I, p. 308, the Grey-Cambon formula became known to the Germans in March 1913. On 10 March 1913 Asquith gave the House of Commons a pledge that there was 'no military engagement to France'. The French ambassador, Paul Cambon, remarked the next day to J. A. Spender, *'la question était maladroite et la réponse était inexacte.'*

CHAPTER TWO

The Balkan Crisis, 1912

IT is extremely difficult to define the meaning of the phrase 'war party', which is so frequently used in discussing German policy before 1914. The expression may be applied to those desiring war immediately, those who might want it in the foreseeable future, or those in favour of gigantic military preparations without specific reference to any political goal. It is very doubtful whether any of the German leaders in 1912 can be classified as members of a 'war party', in the sense that they wanted war that year or next. Prince von Bülow's memoirs say of the Kaiser:

> William II did not want war. He feared it. His bellicose marginal notes prove nothing. His exaggerations were mainly intended to ring in the ears of Privy Councillors at the Foreign Office, just as his more menacing jingo speeches were intended to give the foreigner the impression that here was another Frederick the Great or Napoleon ... William II did not want war, if only because he did not trust his nerves not to give way under the strain of any really critical situation. The moment there was actual danger His Majesty would become uncomfortably conscious that he could never lead an army in the field ...[1]

The Kaiser's nervousness was noted by his contemporaries; the Pan-German Press made contemptuous comments about him during the Agadir crisis, while French newspapers did not improve matters by referring to him as *'Guillaume le Timide'*. The ostentatious chauvinism of the Crown Prince was in some respects a reaction to jibes about his father and references to the declining prestige of the Hohenzollerns.

Whatever criticisms may be directed at Bethmann Hollweg's conduct in July 1914, the evidence is overwhelming that in 1912–13 he favoured a policy of peace. Kiderlen-Wächter appears to have learned his lesson over Agadir; in 1912 his diplomacy was cautious and, with his approval, a retired diplomat

[1] B. von Bülow, *Memoirs 1909–1919* (London, 1932), pp. 148–9.

characterized the Navy League, the Defence League (*Wehrverein*) and the Pan-German League as the greatest obstacles to an effective foreign policy. Although Moltke, the Chief of Staff, frequently indulged in extravagant and bellicose talk, yet he was essentially a weak man with little confidence in his own abilities. Walter Goerlitz notes that Moltke was by nature diffident, had strong intellectual interests and shared with his wife 'an appetite for somewhat exotic forms of religion'. The Chief of Staff believed that his own abilities were sufficient for peacetime requirements but had so little confidence in his capacity to lead the German Army in time of war that 'he actually drew some comfort from the Emperor's frequent declarations that in the event of war he would himself assume command in the west.'[2]

In spite of all his blunders and follies, it is extremely dubious whether Tirpitz can be regarded as a member of a 'war party'. It is true that on occasions he seems to have thought that superior training and gunnery might enable the High Seas Fleet to engage the Royal Navy with some prospect of success, but at no stage before 1914 was this a real tactical possibility. Tirpitz certainly wanted to avoid war in July 1914; moreover his Anglophobia has been much exaggerated. His family were devoted to their English governess and his daughter was sent to school in Cheltenham. Imanuel Geiss has attempted to present Admiral von Müller, Chief of the Kaiser's Naval Cabinet, as a warlike figure. That sombre pessimist and stern critic of the Kaiser may have believed that an Anglo-German war was ultimately inevitable, but his influence on policy was negligible. Responsible German naval opinion in 1912 is reflected in the comments of Admiral von Capelle:

Neither nation wants war. We do not because we are militarily the weaker. England does not because the military and political risk is too great and the reason for fighting is not intelligible to the man in the street.[3]

In a nation of the size and complexity of Germany and among a people steeped in a great military tradition, it is not difficult to find evidence of warlike tendencies. In *Deutschland und der nächste Krieg*, published at the beginning of 1912 and running swiftly through six editions, General von Bernhardi posed

[2] W. Goerlitz, *History of the German General Staff* (New York, 1962), p. 144.
[3] Quoted by M. Balfour, *The Kaiser and his Times* (London, 1964), p. 320.

the alternatives for Germany as 'world power or destruction'. J. McManners has remarked that Germany was 'unfortunate . . . in having a plentiful supply of humourless philosophers and generals who prosaically systematized floating visions of sombre Wagnerian greatness until they took on the air of official prospectuses.'[4] Writings such as those of Bernhardi provide Fischer and members of his school with abundant quotations to justify the thesis of Germany's 'will to world power', but all this evidence must be treated with caution. It is certainly true that from 1911 onwards a stream of imperialist pamphlets poured from the press, while the great victory of the Social Democrats, who emerged from the January 1912 election as the strongest party in the Reichstag, was not necessarily a reverse for imperialism. Charles Andler, Professor of German Literature at the Sorbonne, warned his countrymen: 'The leaders of French Socialism know very well that among the four million who voted for Social Democracy, there are hardly a million real socialists. To the other three million, who are simply discontented democrats, imperialism has great appeal.'[5] Officially the Social Democrats condemned imperialism, but some of their revisionists acknowledged that German workers would gain from larger markets.

An extremely discerning appraisal of the state of German opinion was provided by Colonel Pellé, the military attaché in Berlin, in his report to Millerand, the French Minister of War, on 26 May 1912.[6] He noted the anger over the Agadir settlement, even among Socialists, combined with 'anxiety about a cordon being set up around Germany, and fear of a coalition which may serve to bar the road to the legitimate expansion of the Empire.' Pellé made the interesting comment: 'By anxiety, I do not mean anxiety as to the result of a war; the Germans have no idea of defeat. Their belief in their military superiority is a dogma too firmly held not to have survived even the disappointments of last year.'

The colonel stressed the great interest shown in Bernhardi's theory that war was indispensable to a policy of expansion, combined with the dangerous idea that a war with France was inevitable. His report continued:

[4] J. McManners, *Lectures on European History 1789–1914* (Oxford, 1966), p. 371.
[5] Quoted by H. Goldberg, *The Life of Jean Jaurès* (Madison, 1962), p. 436.
[6] *DDF* 3 III, No. 45.

The militant nationalists (whom we wrongly dub Pan-Germans) are not a mere faction, they pervade the Conservative party, the Ministry of Marine and the army officers. In a military state like Prussia the Army has strong political influence. The military caste permeates the administration, the diplomatic service, the Landtag of Prussia, and forms the entourage of the Sovereign.

Pellé stressed the malign influence of the Crown Prince, and noted: '. . . the Emperor and the Chancellor, who wish to combine the expansion of the Empire with the maintenance of peace, are unpopular.' He concluded:

I repeat that, according to all appearances, the majority of Germans want peace. I am convinced that the 'war party' is today only a small minority. But . . . *one has the impression that this situation may alter rapidly at any moment.* The occasion – the match which may set the fire alight – is liable to arise from some strain between our two countries or from an external happening such as a Balkan crisis.

Contrary to popular belief, Imperial Germany was not a super-militarized state. For many years she had been conscripting barely fifty per cent of her manpower of military age, while France was conscripting over eighty per cent and also drawing heavily on North African manpower. In spite of their great superiority in population – sixty-eight millions against forty millions – the Germans could only count on a slight numerical superiority over the French Army and had to reckon with Russia as well. It was in vain that Schlieffen had urged General von Einem, the very conservative Prussian Minister of War between 1903 and 1909, to consent to army increases essential to the successful application of his plan. Einem believed in superior quality, not superior numbers; he was deeply concerned about the large flow of bourgeois officers into the German Army and considered that any substantial expansion would excessively dilute the quality of the officer corps and undermine the stability of the Prussian State.

By 1912 such ideas were becoming a serious menace to Germany's security. To face a Russian army with a peacetime strength of 1,300,000 men and a French total of nearly 600,000, Austria–Hungary had a peacetime army of 450,000 while Germany could muster some 624,000 men in her standing army. These totals would be tripled on mobilization but, even in trained reserves, France could compete on approximately level terms with Germany. Agadir had increased the confidence of the French Army and military attachés in Paris noted the general expectation of war. Major Winterfeldt, the German attaché, warned his superiors of this in February 1912; in his view French chauvinism was not 'a superficial, temporary phenomenon, but deep-rooted, growing and flourishing'. He noted 'a positive hatred of Germany and a very sensitive national pride'. The changing mood in Paris stimulated the activities of the German *Wehrverein*, founded in 1911 by General Keim with the blessing of Class and the Pan-Germans and dedicated to the immediate strengthening of the German Army.

As a result of discussions between Moltke and General von Heeringen, the Prussian Minister of War, the Reichstag approved measures in May 1912 for raising the strength of the peacetime army from 624,000 to 651,000 men. Two new army corps were established – XX Corps based on Allenstein in East Prussia, and XXI Corps with headquarters at Saarbrücken.[7] According to *The Times*, the law of 1912 'increased enormously the readiness of the Army for war, and was the greatest effort made by Germany since 1870'. Fischer regards this as the initiation of 'a new armaments race', but these significant measures can also be regarded as a belated attempt to remedy Germany's very vulnerable military situation.

Franco-German relations remained tense during the summer of 1912. In French nationalist circles, a new cult of Napoleon looked back to his German triumphs. There was great enthusiasm for aviation and widespread confidence in French superiority in this development. Millerand, the former socialist and now the very chauvinistic Minister of War, sought to stimulate patriotism by great military reviews and torchlight parades at which spectators shouted '*à bas l'Allemagne*'. In September 1912 a crowd in Nancy surrounded the car of Princess Colleredo-Mansfeld, tore off the red, white and black flag and trampled it in the gutter.

The French General Staff was now discarding the cautious defensive plans favoured by the former Chief of Staff, General Michel, and was directing its energies towards the offensive. On 17 January 1912 General Dubail of the *Conseil Supérieur de la*

---

[7] W. Schüssler (ed.), *Weltmachtstreben und Flottenbau* (Witten-Ruhr, 1956), pp. 117–18. There were now twenty-five army corps in the German Army; in addition to the twenty-one numbered corps, there was the Prussian Guard Corps and three Bavarian corps.

Guerre told General Nostiz, the Russian military attaché, that the political situation was very dark and his confidential information was most disquieting. He believed that war would break out in the spring and said, 'we are working as if we are going to have it.' According to Nostiz, Dubail said that, 'alliances are of a defensive nature, and that the art of diplomacy consists in arranging things so as not to appear as the aggressor.' In February General Joffre, the Chief of Staff, told Nostiz that he was preparing for an outbreak of war in the spring. Joffre said: 'All the arrangements for the English landing are made, down to the smallest detail so that the English Army can take part in the first big battle.' At a conference of civil and military authorities held in Paris on 21 February 1912, Joffre proposed to forestall the Germans in case of war by entering Belgium first but Poincaré turned down the request.

France's warlike spirit was greatly stimulated by the close military and naval contacts developing with Britain, but the attitude and strength of her Russian ally aroused some misgiving. In 1910 General Foch told General Wilson that if war broke out in the west, he was far from certain whether Russia would honour the alliance, but Russia would do all that was possible to her if war broke out through the Balkans.[8] Foch was sceptical of the efficiency of the Russians while, during the Agadir crisis, Caillaux remarked to those who urged him to take a strong line, 'you forget that the Russian Army is worth nothing.' Russia was supposed to have embarked on a great programme of military reforms; the size of her standing army and her great masses of trained reserves appeared impressive, but at the Franco-Russian General Staff conference held on 31 August 1911 it was stated that Russia would not be ready for two years to wage war against Germany with the slightest chance of success. At a similar conference on 13 July 1912, the Russian representative, General Jhilinski, stressed the inadequacy of Russia's strategic railways and the slowness of her mobilization. At this conference, Joffre predicted that Germany would commit most of her troops against France and leave only a minimum against Russia. He declared that in the first weeks of the war both France and Russia must launch massive offensives to dislocate the German plan;

[8] J. C. Cairns, 'International Politics and the Military Mind: The Case of the French Republic, 1911–1914', *Journal of Modern History*, September 1953 p. 275.

while recognizing that Russia would have to cope with an Austrian offensive in Poland, he urged that all efforts must be concentrated on annihilating the German armies. Yet Joffre realized that the Russian railways were inadequate, that many important lines would have to be doubled or quadrupled and that much work remained to be done before a major Russian offensive could be launched against Berlin.

The Balkan crisis of 1912 developed against the ominous background of Franco-German tension and great naval and military preparations. Outwardly there was relative calm in the Balkans at the beginning of 1912, but Jules Cambon, the French ambassador in Berlin, commented on 21 January:

... the failing health of the Emperor of Austria, the far-reaching plans attributed to the Heir-Apparent, the Tripoli war, the desire of the Italian Government to extricate itself from the difficulties it has brought upon itself by mixing the disputes of others with its own, Bulgarian ambitions, the threat of trouble in Macedonia, the difficulties in Persia, the shock to the credit of China, all point to serious disorders in the near future ...

The Balkan crisis was precipitated by Russia's renewed interest in the region. Kokovtzov, the very gifted Minister of Finance, who succeeded the murdered Stolypin as Prime Minister in September 1911, was well aware that Russia's vital need was peace and that it was imperative for the Empire to avoid foreign entanglements. Nicholas II was also pacific, but was incapable of exercising effective control. While insisting that foreign affairs were an imperial prerogative with which Kokovtzov had no right to interfere, he allowed his Foreign Ministry to embark on a series of dangerous adventures which could well have touched off a general European war.

The Foreign Minister, Sazonov, was convalescing in Switzerland between March and December 1911, and control of the Foreign Ministry was left in the hands of his assistant, Neratov, a narrow-minded bureaucrat of mediocre abilities. The outbreak of war between Italy and Turkey seemed to threaten the security of the Straits, now a matter of special concern to Russia because of her enormous wheat exports from the Ukraine and her need to import heavy equipment through the Black Sea to further the great programme of industrial expansion then proceeding in south Russia. In October 1911 Charykov, the Russian ambassador in Constantinople, offered to Turkey a guarantee of the status quo in return for opening the Straits to Russian warships. The proposal caused considerable alarm in Constantinople, especially when the ambassador renewed it in November in a form which seemed to presage an ultimatum. Charykov had either misunderstood or exceeded his instructions, and on 9 December Sazonov disavowed him in an interview published in *Le Matin*.

Meanwhile developments of much greater significance were proceeding in the Balkan capitals of Sofia and Belgrade. After the Bosnian crisis of 1909, Izvolski decided to redress the balance in Russia's favour by forming an alliance of the Balkan states. His first step was to appoint Nicholas Hartwig, a rabid Pan-Slav, as Russian minister in Belgrade. As Minister in Teheran, Hartwig had pursued a ruthless policy towards the Persian liberals and had clashed fiercely with his British colleague, but in Serbia he soon gained the confidence of the King, the Heir-Apparent, Prince Alexander, and the Prime Minister, Pasich. On 14 September 1909, the Belgian minister in Belgrade reported that Hartwig had 'become the constant adviser of the Serbian Government which undertakes no measure, makes no decision of any importance, without seeking the decision of the representative of the Tsar in Belgrade'.[9] Hartwig was a formidable and unscrupulous man, and in March 1912 Giers, the Russian ambassador in Vienna, commented unfavourably on his 'incurable Austrophobia'.[10]

With the co-operation of Nekliudov, the Russian minister in Sofia, Hartwig succeeded during the winter of 1911–12 in promoting discussions for a treaty of alliance between Serbia and Bulgaria. Nekliudov, a moderate and level-headed diplomat, visited Sazonov in October 1911 at his convalescent home in Switzerland to seek his approval of the negotiations. Nekliudov records Sazonov's response: 'Well . . . but this is perfect! If only it could come off! Bulgaria closely allied to Serbia in the political and economic sphere; five hundred thousand bayonets to guard the Balkans – but this would bar the road for ever to German penetration, Austrian invasion!'[11]

[9] Quoted by E. C. Helmreich, *The Diplomacy of the Balkan Wars, 1912–1913* (Cambridge, Mass., 1938), p. 28.
[10] E. C. Thaden, *Russia and the Balkan Alliance of 1912* (University of Pennsylvania, 1965), p. 69.
[11] A. Nekliudov, *Diplomatic Reminiscences 1911–1917* (London, 1920), pp. 45–6.

After five months of negotiations, a secret Serbo-Bulgarian treaty was signed on 13 March 1912. The main aim of the agreement was to drive the Turks out of Europe, and provision was made for the division of conquered territory in Macedonia into Serbian and Bulgarian zones. All questions in dispute were to be referred to the arbitration of the Tsar of Russia, and Russia was to be provided with a copy of the treaty. Serbia and Bulgaria undertook to resist with all their forces any attack by Austria, or any attempt by Austria to occupy Turkish territory, including the Sanjak of Novibazar. This agreement was followed by a military convention signed on 12 May 1912, a Græco-Bulgarian treaty on 12 June, and verbal agreements with Montenegro. By September 1912 the Balkan League was poised for the attack on Turkey.

Albertini asks: 'Did Sazonov realize the bearing of these treaties, which could not fail, in the near future, to lead to a war that might spread to the rest of Europe?'[12] Sazonov was not lacking in ability and the British ambassador, Sir George Buchanan, had a high regard for his personal character. He had been very ill in 1911 and was far from fit in 1912, and he frequently displayed a painful inability to come to a decision. Baron Taube, the legal adviser of the Russian Foreign Office, describes him as 'swayed by his feelings, weak, changeable, inexperienced and short-sighted'. He says: 'How many times were his colleagues and subordinates struck by his sudden changes of mind, from one day to another, in the most serious political questions, without apparent reason.' Even strong sympathizers with Russia were often exasperated by the Foreign Minister. Sir George Buchanan wrote on 28 November 1912: 'Sazonov is so continually changing his ground that it is difficult to follow the successive phases of pessimism and optimism through which he passes.' Sir Arthur Nicolson commented on 19 August 1913 'it is impossible to foresee from one day to another what M. Sazonov will do.' Villiers, an official at the British Foreign Office, characterized Sazonov as 'a sad wobbler'.

It is therefore extremely difficult to determine the real aims of Russian policy in 1912. It is certain that Kokovtzov was all for peace, and fortunately his influence on Sazonov was considerable. Nekliudov says of the Prime Minister: 'No one dreaded war for Russia as much as Kokovtsoff, for he was aware both of our lack

[12] L. Albertini, *The Origins of the War of 1914* (London, 1965), I, p. 366.

of military preparation and of the revolutionary ferment which was penetrating ever more deeply into the lower classes and gaining ground daily.' On the other hand Hartwig, who had influential connections with the Russian Foreign Ministry and Court, was playing a reckless and dangerous game in Belgrade, while the chauvinistic press, spearheaded by the widely-read *Novoe Vremya*, appealed to Pan-Slav sentiment and aroused a warlike spirit among the bourgeoisie and nobility. In the summer of 1912 the Grand Duke Nicholas, uncle of the Tsar and commander of the St. Petersburg garrison, paid a visit to France. His ceremonious inspection of forts on the Lorraine frontier, and the anti-German demonstrations of his wife, a daughter of the King of Montenegro, called forth a protest from Berlin. The aggressive confidence of the French General Staff was infecting senior generals of the Russian Army.

In August 1912 Poincaré visited Russia. In April he had learned some particulars of the Serbo-Bulgarian treaty from Izvolski, then ambassador in Paris, but Sazonov now showed him the actual text. Poincaré rightly described it as 'an agreement for war', not only against Turkey but against Austria as well. In his view, it established 'the hegemony of Russia over the two Slav kingdoms'. Sazonov assured him that Serbia and Bulgaria had agreed not to mobilize or declare war without Russian consent, and that Russia could exercise her right of veto to secure the maintenance of peace. According to Sazonov's report, Poincaré said that although no treaty existed between France and England, yet England had given a verbal pledge to aid France with all her land and sea forces if Germany attacked her. Poincaré is said to have expressed misgivings over the failure to inform France about the Serbo-Bulgarian treaty, and regarded it 'as his duty to emphasize that public opinion in France would not allow the Government of the Republic to decide on military action over purely Balkan questions if Germany did not intervene in the conflict and did not, of her own initiative, provoke the application of the *casus foederis*.'

In discussions with Kokovtzov, Poincaré stressed the need to improve Russia's strategic railways and declared that the problem was 'very urgent'. Kokovtzov agreed but drew attention to Russia's financial difficulties. This conversation resulted in very substantial French loans to Russia in 1913.

It cannot be said that Poincaré urged Russia to make war, or to let loose the Balkan states against Turkey in August 1912. Yet he left the initiative to Russia, and Helmreich sums up his attitude as follows: 'France had virtually given Russia a blank cheque on which she might inscribe whatever she wished. Aid was not guaranteed if Russia became involved in a war with Austria–Hungary alone, but both Poincaré and Sazonov knew that Germany would not stand aside in an Austro-Russian conflict.'[13]

On returning to Paris, Poincaré asked the Minister of War for a report on the probable consequences of military intervention by Austria in the Balkans. On 2 September the French General Staff gave their considered opinion that such an intervention would put Germany and Austria 'at the mercy of the Entente'. The General Staff based their view on the argument that Austria would have to employ at least seven of her sixteen army corps in the Balkans, that this would fatally weaken her forces deployed against Russia in Galicia, and that because of the relative weakness of the German forces in East Prussia, the Russians would be able to mount '*une offensive très dangereuse dans le direction de Berlin*'. If the Germans strengthened their forces on the Eastern Front, the French Army with British support would enjoy a substantial superiority in Lorraine; moreover Austrian action in the Balkans might well lead to a rupture with Italy. The French General Staff doubted whether Germany would permit Austria to indulge in a Balkan adventure but, if she did, a general war would result in which 'the Triple Entente would have the best chances of success and might gain a victory which would enable the map of Europe to be redrawn.'[14] On 13 September Poincaré circulated the report to the French ambassadors in London, Berlin, Vienna, Rome, Constantinople and St. Petersburg.

Speaking to Izvolski on 12 September, Poincaré declared that if Serbia attacked Turkey, he expected that Austria would go into action against Belgrade. This might force Russia to undertake military intervention against Austria; France could only give diplomatic support unless Germany entered the fray. Speaking with what Izvolski reports as 'his accustomed gravity of manner', Poincaré said: 'France is unquestionably peace-loving; she neither seeks nor desires a war, but the intervention of Germany against Russia would immediately alter this frame of mind.' He added that 'the experts viewed the chances of the Dual Alliance [i.e.

[13] Helmreich, p. 149.
[14] *DDF* 3, III, No. 359.

France and Russia] in a general outbreak with great optimism.'[15]

It would be imprudent to deduce from these reports and conversations that Poincaré deliberately wanted to bring about a great European war in the autumn of 1912. He was certainly playing for very high stakes, and his policy was both daring and astute. Poincaré knew very well that a victory for the Balkan League over Turkey would have profound repercussions on the European balance of power; it would confirm Russian ascendancy in the Balkans and gravely undermine the security of Austria. Poincaré also knew that Russia was not yet ready for war and he hoped to achieve his aims without touching off a great European conflagration. But he was prepared to run the risk of a general war, even in 1912, and he was encouraged by the optimistic calculations of Joffre and the French General Staff.

The impending crisis in the Balkans was now arousing the attention of Austria and Germany. The Balkan alliance posed a deadly threat to the Central Powers, but both Kiderlen-Wächter and his Austrian opposite number, Count Berchtold, were slow to appreciate the danger. Kiderlen's health was deteriorating seriously in 1912, while Berchtold was new to his post and inclined to hesitation and caution. Berchtold remained ignorant of the Serbo-Bulgarian treaty until the end of May, when Kiderlen told him about it during a visit to Berlin. Neither of the Foreign Ministers were particularly alarmed, for they were both convinced that Russia's internal problems would compel her to pursue a peaceful policy for many years; moreover, they were only aware of the general outline of the treaty. A meeting of Kaiser and Tsar at Baltic Port in July 1912 seemed to confirm Russia's pacific intentions.

Convinced that Russia did not want war and could be relied upon to veto aggressive action by the Balkan League, Kiderlen and Berchtold were inclined to let matters drift. On 13 August, without consulting Kiderlen, Berchtold proposed to the Powers that Turkey should be urged to introduce reforms in her European

---

[15] Albertini, I, p. 373. In *Au Service de la France*, Vol. II. (Paris, 1926), Poincaré angrily repudiated Izvolski's reports of his conversations but, as Thaden remarks (p. 117), 'it is highly questionable whether Izvol'skii would have deliberately falsified Poincaré's statements and intent over a period of months.' Actually *DDF* supports Izvolski's versions and, as Albertini says, there was little in Poincaré's utterances to Russian diplomats between August and November 1912 'of a nature to deter Russia and the Balkan States from risky ventures'.

provinces. This feeble *démarche* aroused little response and irritated Kiderlen. Nor did Berchtold receive any guidance from Bethmann Hollweg when he visited him at Buchlau on 7/8 September, for the Chancellor said 'that he was not a professional diplomat and was not versed in diplomatic phraseology'. He merely advised Berchtold to keep in close touch with Berlin. At an Imperial Council held in Vienna on 14 September, it was agreed that 'any action which might involve Austria in a war was to be avoided.'

The Austrian General Staff did not share Berchtold's passive indifference to the impending storm. The fiery Conrad had been dismissed from his post as Chief of Staff in November 1911 for advocating a preventive war with Italy, but his replacement, General Schemua, demanded on 28 September that Austria should order partial mobilization immediately Serbia declared war on Turkey. He considered that it was essential for Austria to re-occupy the Sanjak of Novibazar and prevent a junction between Serbia and Montenegro. But Berchtold rejected this advice and stated on 2 October that 'only the development of events in the theatre of war can reveal how our interests in the Balkans are affected by the failures or successes on the one side or the other.'

In fairness to the Austrian Foreign Minister, it appeared at the end of September that Russia was resolved to prevent a Balkan war, and was prepared to co-operate with Austria in doing so. Sazonov was then on a visit to Britain and France; Grey met him at Balmoral and was unfavourably impressed by his low vitality and inability to get to grips with details. Grey commented: 'I was afraid that he might want us to take a very strong pro-Balkan and anti-Turk line. Instead of that, however, he was very emphatic about putting strong pressure on the Balkan states to keep the peace, and he did not ask for any peremptory language in Constantinople.' In Paris Sazonov succeeded in persuading Poincaré to propose to the Powers on 4 October that no changes in the status quo in the Balkans would be permitted, although Turkey was to be asked to undertake reforms. Indeed both Sazonov and Izvolsky declared in Paris that if war broke out it would be better if Turkey were victorious, because a big Serbo-Bulgarian success would lead to Austrian intervention.

But it was now too late to stop the Balkan states going to war, and they were encouraged to do so by Russians who opposed official policy. In Belgrade Hartwig told the Serbian leaders not to worry about 'foolish Sazonov', and assured them that they might rely on Russian public opinion and material support. Colonel Romanovski, the military attaché in Sofia, urged the Bulgarians to go ahead. Nelivdov, the director of the Russian Press Bureau, told correspondents that 'the intervention of Russia in the war would be unavoidable, and mentioned that public opinion would force the government to intervene; it was unthinkable that Russia would not help the Balkan states to obtain an expansion of territory.' Early in October the Russian General Staff ordered a 'trial mobilization', which involved a wide calling up of reserves in Russian Poland. Helmreich says:

The suspicion of the Austrian officials that there was a connection between the Russian mobilization and the events in the Balkans was justified. Taube holds there was a direct relation. He is of the opinion that the military, who did not recognize the authority of Sazonov, thought that peace could no longer be maintained in the Balkans, and had taken advantage of the Foreign Minister's absence to obtain the consent of the Tsar for a trial mobilization.[16]

Everything now hinged on the attitude of Germany, and it seems inconceivable that neither the Kaiser, Bethmann Hollweg nor Kiderlen-Wächter should have appreciated the gravity of the impending crisis or the magnitude of the peril now threatening their Austrian ally. Yet the Kaiser wrote on 4 October: 'I will keep out of it. . . . Let them get on with their war undisturbed. . . . If they [the Balkan states] smash the Turks, then they will have right on their side and are entitled to some reward. If they are beaten, they will sing small. . . .' It is true that most military experts expected the Turks to win, but General Schemua thought otherwise and warned Berchtold of the improbability of a Turkish victory.[17]

Events now followed with bewildering rapidity. On 8 October Montenegro declared war on Turkey, and on the 15th the Turks signed an armistice with Italy. On 17 October Serbia, Bulgaria and Greece declared war. On 22/23 October the Bulgarians

[16] Helmreich, p. 159.
[17] Prince von Bülow comments on German policy: 'With a little more skill and foresight it should have been possible to prevent the war in the Balkans. A cold douche turned on Sofia would have been quite enough to stay King Ferdinand, a cautious and never aggressive monarch . . . But we did nothing at all, neither in Belgrade, nor yet in Athens; above all nothing in Sofia, and the Turks were rather encouraged than dissuaded: Bülow, *Memoirs 1909–1919*, p. 111.

smashed the Turkish army in Thrace at Kirk Kilise and drove it back into the Chatalja lines covering Constantinople. On the 24th the Serbs crushed the Turkish forces in Macedonia at Kumanovo. By the end of October the Sanjak of Novibazar had been completely overrun by Serbia and Montenegro, and on 8 November the Greeks entered Salonika. By the end of November the Turks had been driven out of the whole of Europe apart from Constantinople, the Gallipoli peninsula and the fortresses of Scutari, Adrianople and Janina.

The Turkish defeats can be ascribed to inferior numbers, equipment and training; indeed many recruits broke their noses because they did not know how to fire their rifles. Nevertheless the Turks would have fared much better if their High Command had adhered to the plan drawn up by General von der Goltz in 1908; this envisaged a retreat by their Thracian army to a strong defensive line and a withdrawal by their Macedonian forces into the Albanian mountains, pending the arrival of large reinforcements from Asia. At the last moment, the Turkish High Command threw the plan overboard and decided to fight a series of encounter battles in the open.

Taylor says: 'The victory of Balkan nationalism was a disaster beyond remedy for the Habsburg Monarchy.' This was fully appreciated by the Austrian General Staff; on 18 October Schemua submitted a long memoir to Berchtold in which he urged intervention in the Balkans regardless of the risk of a Russian reaction and stated that, even in a single-handed duel with Russia, Austria's chances were 'not at all unfavourable' so long as Serbia and Montenegro were engaged in war with Turkey. In later years a legend arose that Germany had restrained Austria from going to war in October 1912. The truth is that Berchtold was hoping for Turkish successes and preferred to wait until internal squabbles disrupted the Balkan League. But on 25 October, on the morrow of the Serbian victory at Kumanovo, he decided that Serbia should be allowed to extend her influence over areas inhabited by Slavs provided she agreed to an economic *rapprochement* with Austria–Hungary.

Berchtold's policy has been bitterly criticized by Albertini, who argues that Austria could have re-occupied the Sanjak of Novibazar and asserted her ascendancy in the central Balkans without precipitating a war with Russia.[18] Helmreich, on the

[18] Albertini, I, pp. 388–90.

other hand, believes that if Austrian troops had entered the Sanjak, they would have been attacked by the Serbs and that Russia would have come to Serbia's support. In fact it is very doubtful whether Kokovtzov and Sazonov would have been able to resist the pressure for war from the Russian General Staff or the surge of public opinion, elated by the victories of the Balkan League.

In France the victories of the Balkan League were hailed as successes for French arms and training and as triumphs for Creusot over Krupps and Skoda. Yet perceptive observers were appalled at the risk to European peace and Jaurès declared on 16 October: 'Let war once begin and it will spread like a plague into the most terrible holocaust since the Thirty Years War.' *Le Gaulois* commented: 'The state of war in the Balkans constitutes a permanent danger to the peace of Europe. A very fragile thread, which the slightest imprudence may break, supports the sword of Damocles.'

On 27 October Poincaré spoke at Nantes and indicated that the Balkan states should be allowed to retain their conquests. His statement that 'France does not want war and does not fear it', was warmly applauded in the Paris Press. If possible he wished to avoid a general conflict but, as Helmreich says, he 'worked ardently for the diplomatic success of Russia and for the success of the Balkan states.' To Izvolsky he repeated his assurances of full support in a major crisis and declared that 'if Germany supported Austria, France would march.'

In Germany Kiderlen is said to have been 'stupefied by the news of Kirk Kilise', but the Kaiser would not hear of stopping the victorious march of the Balkan armies. The Press displayed a general wish to localize the war, and the *Berliner Neueste Nachrichten* declared, 'so far as we are concerned, we cannot possibly desire a European war for the sake of the Balkans.' The Social Democrats published an appeal calling for mass demonstrations against war. It met with an extraordinary response throughout Germany and drew a crowd of 250,000 at a Berlin meeting on 21 October. Poincaré was even praised in Right-wing newspapers as a 'good European', who was doing his best to keep the peace. Early in November there was a change of mood, and the Catholic *Germania* asserted on the 5th that France was ready 'to place herself at the service of a Pan-Slavic policy and to pull Russia's chestnuts out of the fire'.

On 5 November Berchtold made a statement to the Austro-Hungarian Delegations at Budapest: 'We are ready to take into consideration the new situation created by the victories of the Balkan states and so establish a basis for permanent friendly relations with those states.' But the Foreign Minister torpedoed his own policy by refusing to accept a Serbian port on the Adriatic, and by insisting on the creation of a new state of Albania to block Serbian access to the sea. This was a very inadequate substitute for the bold measures demanded by the Austrian General Staff, but Berchtold felt that something must be done to salvage the Monarchy's prestige. At the end of October Austria began to call up reservists in Bosnia and take military measures on the Serbian frontier. Meanwhile Sazonov was vacillating in typical style; his principal anxiety at this time was that the Bulgarians would capture Constantinople and deprive Russia of her historic goal, and he was not reassured until 18 November when the Bulgarian attacks on the Chatalja lines were repulsed with heavy loss. Sazonov endorsed the Serbian demand for an Adriatic port, but did not press it with energy. Italy indicated her support for an independent Albania.

Berchtold's policies were arousing bitter criticism in Vienna and on 18 November Tschirschky, the German ambassador, summarized the impressions among journalists in the capital:

'We are stumbling into war. If we went consciously with the healthy intention of maintaining our position as a Great Power, taking the South-Slav question in hand and settling it as it suits us, the greater part of the population of the Monarchy would be behind the Government. But one has the feeling that it is yielding step by step from weakness, and this produces a feeling of uncertainty and deep despondency.' At General Staff Headquarters our military attaché was told by one of the leading officers: 'We are ashamed of ourselves. And if we do not pull ourselves together we must draw the consequences and abdicate as a Great Power . . .'

In these circles, as throughout the nobility, there are no illusions as to the gravity of the moment and the momentousness of events in the Balkans for the future of the Monarchy. With amazement and anguish one watches the sudden surge of the Slav breaker, and on all lips hovers the anxious question: what is to become of Austria . . .?

On all sides I hear the question ventilated, whether it will be possible – if the Monarchy does not pull itself together and take vigorous measures against Serbian aspirations and pretensions – to keep the seven million South Slavs in the framework of the Monarchy.

General Auffenberg, the Austrian Minister of War, remarked at an Imperial Council on 19 November: 'We shall see how Russia reacts to our border measures. If she accepts them quietly, then we shall have a free hand against Serbia.' The Archduke Franz Ferdinand and General Schemua were sent to Berlin to consult with the Kaiser and German leaders.

On 7 November Wilhelm II had written to Kiderlen that he saw 'no danger to Austria's existence or even prestige from a Serbian harbour on the Adriatic'. On 9 November Kiderlen had a talk with the Kaiser who declared that he could not 'make himself answerable to his conscience and to his responsibility before God and his people for gambling with the very existence of Germany' on the grounds that 'Austria does not want to have the Serbs in Albania or Durazzo.' In the Kaiser's view 'the alliance did not pledge Germany to support Austria unconditionally in cases of friction over the possessions of others.' He would only recognize the *casus foederis* if Russia attacked Austria without provocation.

On 15 November Serbian troops reached the Adriatic, and the Belgrade Government, encouraged by Hartwig, asserted its claim to an Adriatic port. The Kaiser began to waver, and he used very different language to Franz Ferdinand and General Schemua on 22 November. To Franz Ferdinand, he was 'especially gracious', and the Archduke reported to Vienna that the Kaiser had stated that 'as soon as our prestige demanded it we should take energetic action against Serbia, and we could be certain of his support.' According to Count Szögyeny, the Austrian ambassador, Wilhelm declared that to protect Austria's prestige 'he would not even fear a world war and that he would be ready to enter into a war with the three Entente powers.' According to Schemua, Moltke 'emphasized again and again' that Austria could absolutely count on German support if threatened from Russia. On 2 December Bethmann Hollweg stated publicly in the Reichstag: 'If our allies, in the maintenance of their interests, are, against all expectation, assailed from a third quarter, we shall have resolutely to take our place beside them, in fulfilment of our allied pledge.'

It therefore appears that if Russia had resorted to military measures in support of Serbia's claim to an Adriatic port then a world war would have broken out in 1912. In fact the risk of Russia resorting to such measures was very great, and in the latter part of November Europe was on the verge of a major catastrophe.

From the onset of the crisis, the Russian Ministry of War and General Staff had shown a disposition to play with fire. In October they had ordered the highly provocative 'trial mobilization' in Russian Poland, and early in November they decided to retain with the colours some 400,000 conscripts eligible for release. The Tsar was then at his hunting lodge at Spala in Poland and, in the opinion of the British ambassador, 'the presence of the Grand Duke Nicholas and other generals at the Imperial shooting party ... had tended to give a chauvinistic turn to his policy.'[19] On returning to Tsarskoe Selo, Nicholas listened too readily to the proposals of General Sukhomlinov, his highly irresponsible Minister of War.

Sukhomlinov had held his post since 1909 and has been given credit by Winston Churchill for his role in building up the Russian Army. It is true that important reforms were achieved during Sukhomlinov's period of office, but it seems that most of the credit should go to his assistant, General Polivanov, described by the British military attaché, as 'the best military organizer in Russia'. In any case Polivanov was dismissed in May 1912, while Sukhomlinov continued in office until his dismissal and disgrace in 1915.

Maurice de Paléologue gives the following account of Sukhomlinov in August 1914:

There is something about General Sukhomlinov that makes one uneasy. Sixty-two years of age, the slave of a rather pretty wife thirty-two years younger than himself, intelligent, clever and cunning, obsequious towards the Tsar and a friend of Rasputin, surrounded by a rabble who serve as intermediaries in his intrigues and duplicities, he is a man who has lost the power of work and keeps all his strength for conjugal joys. With his sly look, his eyes always gleaming watchfully under the heavy folds of his eyelids, I know of few men who inspire more distrust at first sight.[20]

On 22 November 1912, Sukhomlinov called a conference with the commanders of the Warsaw and Kiev Military Districts at which they decided to mobilize the entire Kiev District, with part of the Warsaw District, and to prepare to mobilize the

[19] G. Buchanan, *My Mission to Russia* (London, 1923), p. 126.
[20] M. Paléologue, *An Ambassador's Memoirs* (New York, 1925), I, p. 83.

Odessa District. This was in fact the embryo of the famous 'partial mobilization' with which Russia dabbled with such disastrous consequences in July 1914. It is true that in November 1912 Austria had put her troops in Bosnia and Dalmatia on a war footing and was strengthening her Galician garrisons at Cracow, Przemysl and Lemberg, but a Russian partial mobilization on the scale envisaged by Sukhomlinov would infallibly have produced Austrian counter-measures on a very large scale and would probably have led to Austrian general mobilization. Under the terms of the Austro-German alliance, Germany would then have been required to order general mobilization. As General Boisdeffre said to Tsar Alexander III in 1892: 'Mobilization means war.'

All the telegrams for the Russian partial mobilization were prepared on 22 November, but the Tsar decided that it would be as well to call a conference of his senior ministers before the orders were despatched. Accordingly Kokovtzov, Sazonov, Rukhov, the Minister of Communications, and General Jhilinski, the Chief of Staff, were summoned to Tsarskoe Selo on 23 November for discussions with the Tsar and Sukhomlinov.[21] Nicholas outlined Sukhomlinov's plan and stressed that the measures were only directed against Austria, and no menace was intended towards Germany. The Tsar said: 'The Minister of War wanted to despatch these orders yesterday, but I asked him to wait another day.' Kokovtzov says in his memoirs:

> We ... looked at each other with the greatest amazement and only the presence of the Tsar restrained us from giving vent to the feelings which animated all of us.
>
> I spoke first, and had to struggle to retain my composure. I stated frankly that the Minister of War and the two commanders apparently did not perceive what danger they were preparing for Russia in planning this mobilization – a danger of war with Austria and Germany, and at a time when in consideration of the state of our national defence every effort should be made to avert this catastrophe.[22]

Sukhomlinov remained silent but the Tsar argued that these were purely measures of precaution directed only against Austria. Nicholas stressed that he wished to avoid war with Germany and denied that precautions directed against Austria alone would

---

[21] Albertini, I, pp. 402–3, wrongly dates this conference on 10 September and gravely underestimates its importance.

[22] V. N. Kokovtzov, *Out of my Past* (London, 1935), p. 345.

lead to war, but Kokovtzov responded that 'no matter what we chose to call the projected measures, a mobilization remained a mobilization, to be countered by our adversaries with actual war.' The Prime Minister concluded with 'an impassioned appeal to the Tsar not to permit the fatal error the consequences of which were immeasurable, since we were not ready for war and our adversaries knew it well.' Sazonov declared that he was 'simply overwhelmed' by the impending catastrophe, and that in any case Russia had no right to order a partial mobilization without consulting France. In the end Nicholas yielded reluctantly to these appeals and cancelled the proposed mobilization.

Shaking Sukhomlinov's hand, the Tsar said to him: 'Now you can go abroad in peace'. Kokovtzov asked Sukhomlinov to what trip the Tsar had referred and says:

Great was our amazement when Sukhomlinov answered in the most unconcerned manner, 'my wife is abroad, on the Riviera, and I am going to visit her for a few days.' To my astonished question [as to] how he could have planned to go abroad while ordering a mobilization, this flighty gentleman replied without a trace of embarrassment, 'Why not? A mobilization does not have to be conducted by a minister of war in person.'

In connection with the proceedings of the conference of 23 November, it is of interest to note that an order from the Russian General Staff to the Warsaw Military District, dated 12 March 1912, laid down that 'the telegram relative to mobilization is to be regarded at the same time as the Imperial command for the opening of hostilities against Austria and Germany.' However, on 21 November 1912 this order was revoked, and the Warsaw District was informed that 'the proclamation of mobilization was not to be regarded as an Imperial order for the opening of hostilities.' This was to be regulated by a special telegram signed by the Minister of War.[23]

Foreign diplomats in St. Petersburg had no idea of the narrow margin by which peace had been preserved, but were struck by

[23] G. Frantz, *Russlands Eintritt in den Weltkrieg* (Berlin, 1924), pp. 234–40. The idea of a Russian partial mobilization was not entirely extinguished by the conference of 23 November 1912; on 4 January 1913 the Kaiser told Admiral von Müller of 'an impertinent Russian threat' passed on to him by General Tatistchev, the Tsar's personal attaché at his Court, that 'if Austria did not demobilize, Russia would mobilize the Kiev District'. W. Goerlitz (ed.), *Der Kaiser: Aus den Tagebüchern des Chefs des Marinekabinetts Admiral Georg Alexander von Müller* (Göttingen, 1965), p. 127.

Sazonov's change of tone. On 25 November Sazonov astonished the Italian chargé d'affaires by saying that Serbia should only try to get a commercial outlet to the Adriatic, and that he had told Belgrade this. Similar assurances were given to Count Thurn, the Austrian ambassador, to whom Sazonov promised that he would keep Hartwig in hand. Thurn reported to Vienna: 'It is only to be hoped . . . that this entirely unbelievable, mild and conciliatory attitude will last.'

Although Balkan affairs were to give rise to grave tensions in the coming months, the risk of a general European war had perceptibly diminished by December 1912. The crisis contained all the ingredients of a great explosion, but the last-minute intervention of Kokovtzov had averted a catastrophe.

CHAPTER THREE

Europe and the Balkan Turmoil, 1912–1914

ON 3 December 1912 Turkey signed an armistice with Serbia, Bulgaria and Montenegro; Greece did not join in as she wished to continue the siege of Janina and maintain her blockade of the Ottoman coasts. A peace conference, sponsored by the Great Powers, opened in London on 16 December but the negotiations broke down at the end of January 1913 and fighting was resumed. On 6 March Janina capitulated to the Greeks, and on the 26th Bulgarian forces, with strong Serbian support, stormed Adrianople after very bloody fighting. All Bulgarian attempts to break through the Chatalja lines were smashed by the Turks, and on 14 April Bulgaria and Turkey agreed to an armistice. Negotiations dragged on in London, and on 30 May Turkey signed a peace treaty by which she relinquished all territory west of the Enos–Midia line to the Balkan states.

These events had not proceeded without grave friction among the Great Powers. Russian newspapers denounced the London Conference; *Swiet* described it as 'worse than Tsushima', while *Novoe Vremya* considered that Russia had suffered a 'diplomatic Mukden'. Sazonov was savagely abused by the Pan-Slavs, and there were rumours that he would be replaced by Hartwig. We know from Kokovtzov's memoirs that the Russian Cabinet was deeply divided. Sukhomlinov asserted that the Army was in 'splendid condition'; Krivoshein, the Minister of Agriculture, thought it was 'high time Russia stopped cringing before the Germans'. Rukhov spoke of growing prosperity and the patriotic sentiment of the peasant masses. Kokovtzov says: 'Most of the ministers had an implicit faith in the might of the Russian people. . . . I, on the other hand, felt that a war would be a catastrophe for Russia, for by comparison with our enemies our army was ill-equipped and poorly led.'[1] In fact, as Poincaré saw clearly enough, the successes of the Balkan League represented a

[1] Kokovtzov, *Out of my Past*, p. 349.

tremendous triumph for Russian policy and were a stunning blow to Germany and Austria.

During the winter of 1912–13 Austria recalled 224,000 reservists to the colours, while Russia retained the 400,000 conscripts due for release at the end of their third year of service. By mutual agreement, however, both countries substantially reduced their forces in March. Conrad was recalled to the post of Chief of Staff in December 1912, and Moltke wrote to him on 10 February 1913: '. . . a European war must come sooner or later in which ultimately the struggle will be one between Germanism and Slavism . . . but the aggression must come from the Slavs.' On 27 February Franz Ferdinand showed Conrad a letter from Kaiser Wilhelm in which he advised that nothing should be done which might lead to a conflict with Russia. The Archduke told Conrad that he shared this opinion and saw no point in going to war over some Albanian goat pastures. He added 'our chief enemy is Italy, against whom there will have to be a war sometime; we must recover Venetia and Lombardy.'[2]

In fact the situation in the Balkans remained full of peril. In London, Grey presided with considerable adroitness over the conference of ambassadors; he got on well with the German ambassador, Prince Lichnowsky, and was glad to demonstrate that Anglo-German co-operation was a practical reality. Kiderlen-Wächter had died of a stroke in December 1912; his successor, Jagow, was a much weaker personality and so Bethmann Hollweg had to assume a larger role in foreign policy. The Chancellor still hoped to reach an agreement with Britain and wrote to Berchtold on 10 February 1913: '. . . . we may look for a new orientation of British policy if we can get through the present crisis without any quarrels. . . . I think it would be a mistake of immeasurable consequence if we attempt a solution by force . . . at a moment when there is even the remotest prospect of entering this conflict under conditions more favourable to ourselves.'

Nevertheless the Balkans remained intractable. Many

[2] Conrad von Hötzendorf, *Aus Meiner Dienstzeit* (Vienna, 1922–5), III, pp. 155–7. The very cautious attitude of the German leaders in January–February 1913 shows the degree of importance which should be attached to the Kaiser's conference of 8 December 1912, described by Geiss, *July 1914*, p. 42 as 'a kind of war council' and an 'important policy-making meeting'. Indeed Admiral von Müller concludes his account of that conference with the comment, 'the result was thus virtually nil'. W. Goerlitz (ed.), *Der Kaiser*, p. 125.

Bosnian volunteers were serving in the Serbian Army and the victory of Kumanovo had profoundly stirred the millions of South
Slavs in the Dual Monarchy. Berchtold was extremely sensitive
about the boundaries of Albania, and was particularly anxious for
the new state to include Scutari, which between January and
April 1913 was closely besieged by Serbian and Montenegrin
troops. On 14 April Sazonov induced Serbia to withdraw her
troops, but on the 23rd Essad Pasha surrendered Scutari to the
Montenegrins. On 24 April Tschirschky reported the reaction in
Vienna:

> You can hardly imagine the mood here. There is a feeling of shame, of
> smothered rage, the feeling of having been led by the nose by Russia and
> her friends. Poor Berchtold is execrated in the sharpest terms. . . . Even in
> German circles the feeling is expressed that the Monarchy would com-
> pletely abdicate as a Great Power, unless it pulls itself together and shows
> that it is determined to defend its life. . . . If the Monarchy does not now
> assert its will, that will be a defeat for the now dominant German race.
> . . . The Slav flood within the Monarchy would then be impossible to
> contain within its banks and the alliance in the long run could hardly be
> maintained.

Berchtold was now compelled to take action; to his great
disappointment Italy would not commit herself, but Germany
promised her support. Count Mensdorff, the Austrian ambassador
in London, made it clear to the conference that Austria was
prepared to expel the Montenegrins from Scutari by force, and
on 4 May an Imperial Council in Vienna discussed the despatch
of an ultimatum to Cetinje. However, on the 3rd King Nicholas
had telegraphed to Grey that he was abandoning Scutari.

As Taylor says, the establishment of Albania was 'a victory, of
a sort, for Austria–Hungary', but Austrian ministers were under
no illusions. On 2 May Count Stürgkh, the Prime Minister,
depicted the internal situation of the Monarchy in gloomy terms
and referred to 'the unprecedented rise of the Balkan states
which had attained the summit of political and national self-
confidence.' He drew attention to the dangerous situation in
Dalmatia, where the mayor of Spalato had been put on trial for
high treason; he also saw ominous signs of unrest in Bosnia. The
War Minister, Krobatin, and the Finance Minister, Bilinski,
could see no solution except the crushing of Serbian independence. Needless to say Conrad von Hötzendorf fully agreed with
this view.

Germany also was taking stock of her position. In December 1912 Moltke drew up a memorandum which assessed the situation in sombre colours. He was quite convinced that Britain would fight beside France, and that the German Army would face greatly superior forces on both the Eastern and Western fronts. He had little hope of effective Italian support, and expressed deep concern about the strategic problems of Austria in the light of the growing power of the Balkan states. With regard to Russia, he said:

At the present moment Russia is still very much behindhand with the reorganization, equipment and arming of her forces, so that for the time being the Triple Alliance need not be afraid of an armed conflict even with her, in spite of her numerical superiority. But when we look forward into the future we must keep present in our minds the fact that in view of the enormous sums Russia is spending on the reorganization of her army she will be stronger with every year that passes.

Moltke considered that it was vital for Germany to make full use of her effective manpower, and insisted that she must adopt a conscription law as rigorous as that of France.[3]

Bethmann Hollweg was quite prepared to support the proposed increases. He had visited Russia in the summer of 1912, and returned with feelings of deep anxiety about her immense natural resources and prodigious reserves of manpower. During the first months of 1913 the Reichstag considered the request of the Ministry of War for the creation of three additional army corps. On 13 March the *Tägliche Rundschau* published an appeal by the *Wehrverein* urging the necessity for great increases in the military establishment. It stated: 'The gravity of the present situation compels us to make up for lost time. No one in his senses can believe that the shifting of power in the Balkans will not have repercussions on the whole European system ... the Habsburg Monarchy will not escape the need to fight for its existence.' In the end the number of army corps in the standing army remained unchanged at twenty-five, although the General Staff made plans to deploy thirteen reserve corps on the Western Front in order to achieve a numerical superiority in the initial clash.

The attitude of the Social Democrats to the proposed army increases was equivocal. While refusing to accept the army estimates, they voted for the supplementary bill enabling the

---

[3] E. Ludendorff, *The General Staff and its Problems* (London, n.d.), I, pp. 57–69. The memorandum was largely inspired by Colonel Ludendorff, then Chief of the Operations Section of the General Staff.

Government to proceed with the proposed military expansion. Bebel declared: 'Nobody in Germany wants to expose a defence-less and weak fatherland to foreign attack . . . the SPD has never denied the imperative need for powerful, well-armed defensive forces.'[4] On 13 July 1913 the Reichstag agreed to the call-up of an additional 72,000 men in October 1913 and another 60,000 in October 1914. This was the largest army estimate in German history and, when completed, would raise the peacetime strength of the Army to nearly 800,000 men. To finance the increases and provide ample reserve stocks of munitions, the Reichstag accepted the extraordinary measure of a capital levy of £50,000,000.

The German programme was matched by even greater pre-parations in France. Poincaré had moved to the Presidency in January 1913, and promptly issued a message to the French nation declaring that it was impossible for a people to be pacific unless they were always ready for war. He demanded great sacrifices to strengthen the French Army and Navy, and in July 1913 the Ministry of Barthou induced the French Chamber to increase the period of military service from two to three years. This had the effect of raising the French peacetime strength by 160,000 men, and gave France a standing army equal if not superior in size to that of Germany.[5] In March 1914 the French Chamber was informed that France had 790,000 men under arms, of whom 245,000 were on her eastern frontier.

In May 1913 the French Supreme War Council adopted Plan XVII, based on the conception of the *offensive à outrance* and inspired by faulty deductions from Napoleon's campaigns. It was designed to smash the Germans in Lorraine and southern Belgium and then thrust across the Rhine in the direction of Berlin. The regulations of October 1913 proclaimed: 'The French Army, returning to its traditions, henceforth admits no law but the offensive.' The French High Command was intoxicated by the great masses which the Three Years Law was placing at its

[4] D. Groh, 'The "Unpatriotic Socialists" and the State', *JCH*, October 1966 p. 166.

[5] It is not possible to give exact comparative strengths of the French and German Armies in 1913–14. Calculations differ and depend on whether the authority concerned is including members of the administrative cadre, one-year volunteers or troops in the colonial empire.

The French 1913 measures are often presented as a reaction to those of Germany; actually they proceeded simultaneously.

disposal and Joffre's deputy, General de Castelnau, proclaimed:
'Give me 700,000 men and I will conquer Europe!'

Franco-German relations remained very uneasy during 1913.
The *Kölnische Zeitung* commented on 10 March, 'never have our
relations with our western neighbour been so tense, never has the
revanche been so bluntly avowed.' On 3 April a Zeppelin crossed
the French frontier and was compelled to land at Lunéville to
refuel; the incident provoked hostile demonstrations. Ten days
later two parties of German tourists were insulted and molested
at Nancy without police interference. An intensive propaganda
campaign, partly inspired by the Army, assured Frenchmen that
in every way they were superior to Germans, and that war in the
future would be decided by lightning blows. Time and again it
was asserted in military journals that the question of Alsace-
Lorraine could only be decided in France's favour by force of
arms. *La France Militaire* declared: 'It will be a beautiful war
which will deliver all the captives of Germanism.'[6]

Yet many Frenchmen declined to be swept along by the tide
of nationalism and militarism. Caillaux opposed the Three Years
Service Law, while Jaurès deplored the deterioration in Franco-
German relations. Close financial ties between French and
German industrialists provided a possible basis for co-operation.
In November 1913 a series of clashes between German soldiers
and civilians in the Alsatian town of Zabern might have inflamed
Franco-German relations but, in general, French newspapers
commented on the affair with restraint and it was left to the
German Reichstag to pass a resolution condemning the conduct
of their Army.

In the summer of 1913 war again flared in the Balkans. Deprived
of gains in Albania, Serbia demanded a larger share of Macedonia;
moreover, while the Bulgarians were exhausting themselves before
Adrianople and the Chatalja lines, Greek and Serbian troops
had occupied much territory promised to Bulgaria in the treaty
of March 1912. Hartwig's advice to the Serbian Government was
plain enough: 'If war must come, Serbia must see that Bulgaria
provokes it.' Increased tension between Bulgaria and her allies
offered a real opportunity to Austrian statesmanship, but the situation was complicated by Rumania's insistence that Bulgaria

[6] Weber, *The Nationalist Revival in France 1905–1914*, p. 127. Incidentally
Taylor, p. 518 *n*. says: 'It is often said that the French projected war in order to
recover Alsace and Lorraine. There is not a scrap of evidence for this.'

should 'compensate' her by the cession of Silistria and part of the Dobruja. Although nominally tied to the Triple Alliance by a secret treaty signed in 1883, Rumania was pursuing an independent line and was bitterly resentful of the treatment of Rumanians in the Hungarian province of Transylvania. Tsar Ferdinand and the Bulgarian General Staff were reluctant to accept Berchtold's advice to make concessions to Rumania; they had little confidence in the proffered arbitration of Nicholas II and were supremely confident that the Bulgarian Army could smash the Serbians and Greeks. On the night 29/30 June, without consulting his Prime Minister, Danev, Ferdinand ordered his troops to attack the Serbian and Greek forces in Macedonia.

Events developed so rapidly that it was virtually impossible for Austria to intervene, even if Berchtold had been capable of a swift decision. After very severe fighting the Battle of Bregalnitza developed into a great Serbian victory and by 8 July the Bulgarians were retreating in disorder beyond their old frontier, while Greek troops overwhelmed the inadequate Bulgarian forces in the Kavala area. On 10 July Rumania declared war; her forces crossed the Danube and marched unopposed on Sofia. On 12 July the Turks attacked in Thrace and on the 22nd recaptured Adrianople. On 21 July Ferdinand telegraphed King Carol of Rumania to ask for peace, and the victorious allies granted him an armistice on the 31st.

At this moment of destiny for the Central Powers, very serious differences developed between Vienna and Berlin. On 1 July Tschirschky reported that, if Bulgaria won a decisive success, Austria might occupy Belgrade. Intervention would also be necessary if Serbia were victorious in order to prevent the creation of a greater Serbia. The Kaiser commented on this: 'Completely crazy; so war after all.' On 3 July Berchtold told Tschirschky that he regarded the situation with grave concern. He said there could be no illusions about the threat which an enlarged Serbia would pose to the Monarchy; if Bulgaria were decisively beaten Austria might have to take military action, with the attendant risk of Russia intervention. In no case could Monastir be allowed to go to Serbia. On 5 July – exactly one year before the famous Potsdam 'blank cheque' – the Kaiser commented that 'it was a serious mistake for Count Berchtold to be unyielding now over Monastir as he had previously been over Durazzo.' On 6 July Bethmann Hollweg discussed the situation with Count Szögyeny, the Austrian ambassador. The Chancellor said:

> How the present hostilities between Bulgaria and Serbia will end, no man knows. One thing, however, is certain, that whether Bulgaria wins or Serbia, both states will be weakened and filled with hatred for each other . . .
>
> If Austria–Hungary were to seek by diplomatic means to eject Serbia from any newly-won territories, she would have no success and would mortally offend Serbia. And, if she attempted to use force, it would mean a European war. This would most seriously affect the vital interests of Germany and I must therefore expect that before Count Berchtold makes any such resolve, he will inform us of it.
>
> I can therefore only express the hope that Vienna will not let its peace be disturbed by the nightmare of a Greater Serbia, but will await further developments in the Bulgarian-Serbian theatre of war. From the idea of wanting to swallow Serbia I can only urgently dissuade the Monarchy, as this could only weaken it.

On 7 July Jagow, the German Foreign Secretary, made the comment: 'Developments in the Balkans are almost beyond expectation favourable to Austria–Hungary: the Balkan League is split, Russian influence has received a severe blow and the Balkan States, now tearing one another to pieces, will be so weakened by the war that they will need a long time to recover.' Such were the views of the Chancellor and Foreign Secretary, whom members of the Fischer school have endeavoured to present as exponents of *Realpolitik* capable of manipulating events in order to bring on a great war, which would establish German hegemony in Europe and the world.

On 10 August 1913 Bulgaria was compelled to sign the Treaty of Bucharest, by which Serbia acquired most of Macedonia, while Greece obtained Kavala and a large slice of western Thrace. Bulgaria ceded her share of the Dobruja to Rumania, together with the important town of Silistria. By a separate treaty at the end of September, Turkey regained Adrianople. Bulgaria had to be content with access to the Aegean Sea; whereas she only gained 400,000 new subjects, both Serbia and Greece had increased their population by a million and a half. On 7 August the Kaiser congratulated King Carol on the 'splendid success' of his 'wise and statesmanlike policy', and on the same day he declared that Vienna had 'gone completely crazy', because Berchtold objected to the settlement. In expressing these views, the Kaiser was strongly influenced by his personal dislike of Ferdinand and his own family connections with the royal houses of Rumania and Greece.

Austrian foreign policy had now reached a desperate *impasse*. Count Tisza, the masterful Prime Minister of Hungary, would make no concessions in Transylvania to conciliate Rumania; at the same time he was opposed to a war with Serbia which might increase the number of Slavs in the Monarchy. The Archduke Franz Ferdinand, on the other hand, detested the Magyar magnates, and was anxious to win over Rumania. Whatever his views on the South Slav question, the Archduke was not in favour of war with Serbia.[7] While Conrad von Hötzendorf regarded Serbia as a mortal foe who must be crushed at the first opportunity, the old Emperor Franz Josef only wanted to end his days in peace. The German Government showed little understanding of Austria's racial problems and, in the circumstances, it would have required a far abler statesman than Berchtold to pursue a coherent foreign policy.

The Treaty of Bucharest had hardly been signed, when a new crisis arose in the Balkans. Disregarding the decisions of the London Conference, the Serbs continued to maintain troops on Albanian territory; moreover, in Macedonia the oppressive Serbian military occupation, far from winning over the local population, had alienated it by a series of atrocities. A fierce revolt broke out in late September and the widely scattered Serbian forces were hard put to hold their own against Albanian and Bulgarian partisan bands. Serbian reinforcements gained the upper hand and advanced deep into Albania in pursuit of the 'rebels'; at the same time the Serbian Government demanded a frontier rectification. After much hesitation and various conferences in Vienna, Berchtold requested the Serbs to withdraw on 14 October, but the Prime Minister, Pasich, returned an evasive reply. Fay considers that he was being influenced by Hartwig and 'by subterranean pressure from the secret society of Serbian military officers known as the "Black Hand"'.[8] Berchtold now decided on stronger measures.

[7] V. Dedijer, *The Road to Sarajevo* (London, 1967), pp. 131–41 disputes the traditional view that the Archduke wanted to establish 'trialism' and make the South Slavs a third unit of the Monarchy.

[8] S. B. Fay, *The Origins of the War of 1914* (New York, 2nd edition revised 1966), pp. 470–1.

Sazonov was then in Paris and agreed with the French Foreign Minister, Pichon, that the Serbian attitude was indefensible and in flat contradiction to the decisions of the London Conference – it may well be that Sazonov and Pichon appreciated that it would be most unwise to pick a quarrel with Austria over an issue in which Grey's sympathies were bound to be with the Dual Monarchy. Meanwhile Berchtold had asked for German support and on 16 October the Under-Secretary, Zimmermann, replied that 'in the efforts made to secure an autonomous Albania we firmly back Austria–Hungary.' Zimmermann reported this development to the Kaiser, who was then at Leipzig attending the centenary celebrations of the Battle of the Nations. He reacted with characteristic violence – possibly swept along by the wave of patriotic fervour by which he was surrounded – and told Conrad, who was attending the celebrations, that strong measures must be taken against Serbia. Wilhelm declared on 18 October:

I go with you. The other [Powers] are not prepared, they will not do anything about it. In a few days you would be in Belgrade. I was always a supporter of peace, but there are limits. I have done much reading about war and know what war means, but finally the situation occurs, in which a Great Power can no longer look on, but must reach for the sword.

Berchtold was unaware of this conversation when he despatched an ultimatum to Serbia on 18 October, and gave her a week to withdraw her troops from Albania, 'otherwise Austria would be forced, with regret, to have recourse to the proper measures to secure the realization of her demands.' Fay says: 'At Belgrade Pasich and Hartwig learned of the ultimatum with rage and dismay, especially as it was soon followed by strong warnings from all the Great Powers, now suddenly awakened to the possible danger of serious complications . . .' Pasich had no alternative but to yield, but declared that he was doing so 'not under pressure of Austria, but out of regard for the friendly advice of Russia'.

The Kaiser now came to Vienna and on 26 October had a long conversation with Berchtold, who quotes him as saying: '. . . if His Majesty Emperor Franz Josef requires something, the Serbian Government must comply and, if it fails to do so, Belgrade shall be bombarded and occupied until the will of His Majesty has been carried out.' The Kaiser declared that he was fully prepared to draw the sword in support of Austria, and accompanied these words by clapping his hand on his sword-hilt. Fischer attaches much importance to this conversation and describes it at length. Albertini, on the other hand, suggests that Berchtold regarded the Kaiser 'as a nit-wit on whom it was not worth while to waste time and breath'.

The troubled year 1913 witnessed a further crisis in November, when Sazonov learned of the appointment of General Liman von Sanders, head of the German Military Mission to Turkey, to command the First Ottoman Army Corps in Constantinople. He jumped to the conclusion that the General had been 'entrusted with the task of firmly establishing German influence in the Turkish Empire'. In fact Sazonov greatly exaggerated the importance of the mission; the General – who incidentally was of Jewish ancestry, a rare thing among Prussian generals – had been specially told by the Kaiser to stay out of politics. Ulrich Trumpener says: '. . . Liman concluded that his primary task was to reform the Ottoman army, not to serve as an agent for the German Foreign Office or German business interests.'[9] In fact his role was exactly similar to that of Admiral Limpus, head of the British Naval Mission to Turkey. At Sazonov's request, Kokovtzov spoke to the Kaiser and Bethmann Hollweg about the affair when he passed through Berlin in mid-November; he received conciliatory replies and the Kaiser expressed his readiness to see whether Liman could be given command of an army corps other than that of Constantinople.

These assurances failed to appease the volatile Sazonov; he appealed for the support of Britain and France and declared that 'this matter would be a test of the value of the Triple Entente.' To the Tsar he complained on 6 December: 'To abandon the Straits to a powerful state would be synonymous with subordinating the whole economic development of southern Russia to that state.' Delcassé, now French ambassador at St. Petersburg, encouraged Sazonov to adopt a strong line, but Grey's response to Sazonov's requests was decidedly cool.

On 13 January 1914 an Imperial Russian Council discussed the imposition of military or diplomatic measures against Turkey. Sazonov admitted that British support was uncertain, but that

[9] U. Trumpener, 'Liman von Sanders and the German-Ottoman Alliance', *JCH*, October 1966, p. 180. See also H. S. W. Corrigan, 'German-Turkish Relations and the Outbreak of War in 1914: a Reassessment', *PP* April 1967. Fischer, *Germany's Aims in the First World War*, pp. 45–6 completely misinterprets the significance of Liman's mission.

Delcassé had assured him, 'France will go as far as Russia wishes.' Admiral Grigorovich, the Navy Minister, thought it would be possible to occupy Trebizond under cover of naval bombardment, and to hold it as a pledge until Turkey revoked Liman's appointment. Kokovtzov declared that this would lead to war with Germany and asked: 'Is war with Germany desirable and can Russia wage it?' Sukhomlinov and Jhilinski, the Chief of Staff, 'categorically declared that Russia was perfectly prepared for a duel with Germany, not to speak of one with Austria'. Kokovtzov reiterated his opinion that 'a war at present would be the greatest misfortune that could befall Russia.' The Council adopted his view and decided to endeavour to reach a settlement by negotiation.

Two days later Germany accepted a compromise; Liman von Sanders was appointed Inspector-General of the Turkish Army but gave up his command of the Constantinople corps. On 16 January the Russian ambassador in Berlin reported that 'the Berlin Cabinet had done all in its power to satisfy our legitimate wishes, not an easy thing in view of the Press campaign directed against the Government.' This was the end of the affair, although a Russian commission, meeting on 21 February, reported glaring deficiencies in the Black Sea Fleet which was certainly in no condition to support amphibious operations against Turkey.

Influenced by reactionary circles at Court, the Tsar dismissed Kokovtzov from his post at the end of January and replaced him by Goremykin, whom Sir George Buchanan describes as 'an amiable old gentleman, with pleasant manners, of an indolent temperament and quite past his work.' In the next international crisis, Russia would have to rely on the mercurial Sazonov, guided by such advice as he might receive from her ignorant and irresponsible military chiefs.

CHAPTER FOUR

The Eve of War, 1914

THE outcome of the Balkan Wars had disastrous effects on Austria's strategic position. Serbia was now a formidable military power, capable on mobilization of putting 200,000 men in the field, backed by more than 200,000 reserves and, in the event of war with Russia, Conrad would have to send substantial forces towards the Danube frontier. Rumania had now changed from a potential ally into a very doubtful neutral, which meant that Conrad could no longer count on some 400,000 Rumanian troops, who were supposed to cover the right flank of the Austrian armies in Galicia.

The Austrian Chief of Staff was under no illusions and summed up the position in a memorandum dated 16 January 1914:

> Serbia and Rumania have thus become the nearest dangerous enemies of the Monarchy and are therein supported by Russia and France; the Triple Entente has thereby achieved a preponderance . . .
>
> It can be said in advance that with a constellation such as France, Russia, Rumania, Serbia and Montenegro on the one hand and Austria–Hungary, Germany and Italy on the other, the military preponderance not only in relative figures, but also in geography lies on the side of the Triple Entente . . .
>
> This will be the case even if Rumania merely remains neutral, while military intervention on her part against the Monarchy would create a highly dangerous preponderance on the enemy side.[1]

Conrad says: 'After the Treaty of Bucharest I ceased to urge war, and indeed attempted to postpone it until our military preparations – the only chance of saving Austria – improved.' In March 1914 Austria increased her annual levy of recruits from 175,000 to 200,000 men, thus raising the strength of her standing army to 475,000. This increase appears trivial when compared with the vast military programme adopted by Russia at the end of 1913. This was intended to add 500,000 men to her standing

[1] Conrad, *Aus meiner Dienstzeit*, III, p. 757. By June 1914 Conrad had become much more pessimistic about Italy.

army and raise it to a total of over 2,000,000 in 1917. Great sums were allotted by the Duma to augment the artillery and reserve stocks of munitions, while a French loan of 200,000,000 roubles was being devoted to the development of strategic railways in western Russia. In August 1913 Joffre visited Russia and Delcassé reported to Paris that the French Chief of Staff was very satisfied with the progress in railway construction and impressed by the growing efficiency of the Russian Army.

The changing power structure in the Balkans and the massive increases in Russia's military strength made it very doubtful whether Austria would be able to fulfil the role allotted to her in the plans of the German General Staff. Profoundly sceptical of the efficiency of the Austrian Army, Schlieffen had deliberately refrained from discussing plans with his colleagues in Vienna, but in January 1909 Moltke gave Conrad an outline of the Schlieffen Plan. He told him that Germany would have to concentrate first on crushing France, and only then could the bulk of her forces be transferred to the Eastern Front. Moltke realized that the German Eighth Army in East Prussia would not suffice to hold back the Russian masses, and welcomed the plan for a formidable Austrian thrust from Galicia in order to tie down the bulk of the Russian Army. To encourage Conrad, he gave him the impression that the German Eighth Army would be strong enough at the outset to launch an offensive from East Prussia against the Russian railway communications running east of Warsaw.[2]

Moltke fully appreciated that a hostile Serbia constituted a very serious complication, and his particular anxiety was that a substantial part of the Austrian Army would become entangled in an invasion of Serbia, thus weakening the vital Austrian offensive in Poland. He was very worried by the possibility that, in the event of an Austro-Serbian War, Russia would take no action until the Austrians had committed large forces towards the Danube. In 1909 Moltke agreed with Conrad that 'the most likely and the most dangerous case would be a Russian intervention after war with Serbia had begun.' Faced with this dilemma, Conrad prepared two mobilization plans – Plan R

[2] For Austro-German strategic planning see N. Stone, 'Moltke and Conrad: Relations between the Austro-Hungarian and German General Staffs, 1909–1914', *HJ*, No. 2, 1966.

('Russia') by which thirteen army corps took the field against Russia, while three corps stood in readiness against Serbia; and Plan B ('Balkan'), which involved a partial mobilization and offensive against Serbia with seven corps, combined with an eventual defensive against Russia with nine corps if a general mobilization became necessary. As Plan B ran directly counter to the Schlieffen Plan, it was an anathema to Moltke, but Conrad had no love for the Germans and was quite prepared to implement it. But even the successful application of Plan R was becoming extremely doubtful in 1914, in view of the enormous forces which Russia would be able to deploy in southern Poland and the probable absence of any distraction in Austria's favour by Rumania. Moreover Colonel Redl, Chief of Staff of the Prague army corps, who committed suicide in May 1913, had betrayed the Austrian plans to the Russians.

In 1911 Moltke introduced substantial modifications to the Schlieffen Plan. Schlieffen had intended to lure the French into an offensive towards the Rhine and argued that the deeper they penetrated into Germany, the more certain would be their destruction at the hands of the German right wing sweeping through Belgium and Holland. Moltke shrank from this bold and imaginative strategy and, by planning to deploy two powerful armies in Lorraine, completely altered the balance between the German right and left wings. Moreover, he decided to abandon the projected sweep through Holland and wrote: '. . . it will be very important to have in Holland a country whose neutrality allows us to have imports and supplies. She must be the windpipe that enables us to breathe.' Apart from the threat of blockade, Moltke considered that 'a hostile Holland at our back could have disastrous consequences for the German Army in the west.' Moltke's memorandum continued:

However awkward it may be, the advance through Belgium must therefore take place without the violation of Dutch territory. This will hardly be possible unless Liège is in our hands. The fortress must therefore be taken at once [i.e. at the very beginning of mobilization]. . . . Everything depends on meticulous preparation and surprise. The enterprise is only possible if the attack is made at once, before the areas between the forts are fortified. It must therefore be undertaken by standing troops immediately war is declared . . . the possession of Liège is the *sine qua non* of our advance.[3]

[3] Ritter, *The Schlieffen Plan*, p. 166. See map 3, p. 87, Schlieffen in 1905 intended to mask Liège with two Landwehr brigades.

By abandoning the wide sweep through Holland, Moltke was imposing a tremendous logistical burden on the German First and Second Armies destined to advance north of the Meuse. Until Liège was taken, its outer forts shattered and its four lines of railway brought under German control, no advance into the Belgian plain would be possible. More than 600,000 men must pass through this bottleneck and everything hinged on its capture in the first days of the war. Accordingly six brigades of infantry and supporting artillery had to be kept permanently on a war-footing in the Aachen area.

The decision to capture Liège at the outset of the war was kept a close secret by the General Staff, and Bethmann Hollweg did not hear of it until 31 July 1914. Like his predecessor, Bülow, the Chancellor was informed of the general features of the Schlieffen Plan and raised no objection to the contemplated violation of Belgian neutrality, but he should certainly have been told about the *coup de main* against Liège, which was to have the gravest political consequences in 1914.[4] Winston Churchill says:

Nearly three weeks before the main shock of the armies could begin . . . six German brigades must storm Liège. It was this factor that destroyed all chance that the armies might mobilize and remain guarding their frontiers while under their shield conferences sought a path to peace. The German plan was of such a character that the most irrevocable steps of actual war, including the violation of neutral territory, must be taken at the first moment of mobilization. Mobilization therefore spelt war.[5]

Moltke's decision to spare Holland shows that the German General Staff attached far more importance to British intervention than many historians have appreciated. Taylor says: 'Indeed they [the German General Staff] had always assumed that Great Britain would enter the war; they did not take her military weight seriously, and naval questions did not interest them.' So far from this being the case, the potential threat of a British blockade had led Moltke in 1911 to make a very substantial modification in the Schlieffen Plan and one which probably doomed the German campaign in the west before it was

[4] There is a persistent legend that the German General Staff imposed the Schlieffen Plan on the political authorities without prior consultation. For the degree to which the German Government was kept informed see L. C. F. Turner, 'The Significance of the Schlieffen Plan', *AJPH* April 1967, pp. 53–5.

[5] W. S. Churchill, *The World Crisis: The Eastern Front* (London, 1931), p. 93.

ever launched. From the very start of their offensive in August 1914, the German First and Second Armies were faced with chronic supply problems, which they would not have encountered if the railways and roads of southern Holland had been at their disposal. Moltke and his mentor, Ludendorff, committed a fatuous blunder when they decided to try and maintain more than 600,000 men through the narrow aperture of Liège.

It is clear also that Moltke feared that Anglo-Dutch forces might thrust towards the Ruhr, while the German Army was pressing into France. Fischer says of the British Expeditionary Force that 'the soldiers rated the effectiveness of Britain's military contribution low.'[6] On the contrary, Schlieffen in his final memorandum of December 1912 expressed fears that the British might block the line Antwerp–Namur, while in a memorandum drawn up in 1913, Moltke declared that Britain would intervene with a modern, fully equipped army of 132,000 men and said 'as opponents they are not to be underestimated.'[7]

Since British intervention was taken so seriously by the German General Staff, the question of Anglo-German relations in 1912–14 assumes special importance. These had certainly been improving in spite of naval competition. Churchill says: 'The spring and summer of 1914 were marked in Europe by an exceptional tranquillity. . . . Naval rivalry had at the moment ceased to be a cause of friction . . . it was certain that we could not be overtaken as far as capital ships were concerned.'[8] McManners points out that 'the evidence of English trade journals makes it clear that trade rivalry between the two empires did not constitute a threat to peace.' While admitting that Germany, the United States and Japan represented Britain's most dangerous commercial competitors, he says: '. . . they were also her most promising markets, and Germany, from 1911, was the best market of all.'[9] British exports of manufactured goods nearly doubled between 1905 and 1914; although German trade with South America was growing, British exports to that continent were fifty per cent larger in 1912. Britain's mercantile marine still constituted nearly half of the world's tonnage; even if her relative

---

[6] Fischer, *Germany's Aims in the First World War*, p. 38, and Taylor p. 525.
[7] G. Ritter, *Staatskunst und Kriegshandwerk* (München, 1965), II, p. 270.
[8] W. S. Churchill, *The World Crisis 1911–1914* (London, 1923), pp. 178–9.
[9] McManners, *Lectures on European History 1789–1914*, p. 373.

share in world trade was declining, her imperial and economic ascendancy had little to fear from German rivalry.

There was a feeling in Liberal circles that Germany had a real grievance in being denied 'a place in the sun'; this led to an Anglo-German agreement – very favourable to Germany – on the possible partition of the Portuguese colonies. It is true that Grey was reluctant to sign the document, but he would probably have done so if war had not broken out in July 1914. Anglo-German negotiations about the Bagdad railway also made good progress; the German Government overcame objections from the *Deutsche Bank*, which held large concessions in Turkey, and agreed not to extend the railway south of Basra. Plans were also made by the ingenious Sir Ernest Cassel for Anglo-German co-operation in exploiting oil concessions in Mesopotamia. Fischer says:

> The credit for this agreement must go to the German government. . . . The agreements on the railway, the ports on the Persian Gulf and the irrigation of Mesopotamia show how strongly Germany was endeavouring to reach an understanding – and ultimately an alliance – with Britain, even at the cost of sacrifice. In these fields Germany was unmistakably willing to play the junior partner to Britain as a world power.[10]

Economic interests in the Near East also provided a possible basis for understanding between France and Germany. France had a great stake in the Ottoman Empire and French bondholders held sixty per cent of the Turkish debt. Maurice de Paléologue, the Political Director of the French Foreign Office, said to Izvolski in April 1913: 'You want to exhaust Turkey; we want her to be capable of still living and even of recovering in Asia.'[11] Bompard, the French ambassador in Constantinople, urged the need for co-operation with Germany in restoring Turkey. In the spring of 1914 France made a large loan to Turkey in return for substantial concessions. The news aroused misgivings in Berlin, where the Kaiser commented that German influence in Turkey was 'already as good as nil'; he feared that superior French financial strength would draw the Ottoman Empire into the French orbit. Certainly the Berlin money market could not compete with that of Paris, and the *Deutsche Bank* had very great

[10] Fischer, *Germany's Aims in the First World War*, p. 41.

[11] *DDF* 3, VI, No. 222. In fact in May 1914 a Turkish delegation to Nicholas II was angling for an alliance with Russia.

difficulty in floating a loan in June 1914 for extensions to the Bagdad Railway. Fischer attaches much importance to these transactions, but it is difficult to see any connection between them and the outbreak of war. It is an illusion to believe that the Germans were thirsting for an alliance with Turkey in 1914. Alliance negotiations did not begin until 28 July, and Trumpener says, 'it is clear that before the July crisis Germany's leaders were not even sure that an alliance with the Turks was desirable.' In May 1914 Moltke specifically ruled out any alignment with Turkey in the foreseeable future.

Although Franco-German relations remained fairly tense in the first months of 1914, there were indications of a possible change. On 20 January Poincaré accepted an invitation to dine at the German Embassy – the first President to do so since 1871. The influential Caillaux believed that co-operation with Germany in economic and political fields was possible and desirable. He became Minister of Finance in December 1913, and had a real prospect of becoming Prime Minister of a Radical-Socialist coalition. Baron Guillaume, the Belgian minister in Paris, reported early in 1914:

I feel certain that Europe would profit from the policies of M. Caillaux, the Radicals and the Radical-Socialists. As I have already told you, MM. Poincaré, Delcassé, Millerand and their friends have created and pushed the current policies of nationalism, militarism and chauvinism . . . I see in them the greatest threat to the peace of Europe today.[12]

Jaurès declared in 1914: 'The ablest man we have now in France is Caillaux. More than ability, he has will, character and a sense of decision.' Caillaux had opposed the Three Years Service Law and felt that the Russian alliance would drag France into dangerous adventures. He would have agreed with Jules Cambon, who remarked to the Belgian minister in Berlin: 'The great majority of Germans and Frenchmen want to live in peace. . . . But a powerful minority in both countries dreams only of battles, conquests and revenge.' On 20 August 1913, Major Winterfeldt, the German military attaché in Paris, ascribed peaceful sentiments to the majority of the French people.

In June 1914 Caillaux said to Jaurès: 'As soon as possible we must form a Leftist Ministry which will press for a policy of European peace.' However, Caillaux was now out of office. As

[12] Goldberg, *The Life of Jean Jaurès*, p. 446.

a tough and unscrupulous party manager, he had many enemies and the nationalists were directing a ruthless Press campaign against him; in the spring of 1914 *Le Figaro* was publishing confidential letters exchanged with his second wife. Matters reached a dramatic climax on 16 March when Mme Caillaux, desperate at the prospect of further revelations, took a Browning automatic to the offices of *Le Figaro* and fired six deadly shots into the editor, Calmette. This was too much even for French politics and Caillaux immediately resigned. He was still out of office, when his wife was brought to trial in July 1914 and a gallant French jury returned a verdict of 'not guilty'.

Elections in April–May 1914 demonstrated the unpopularity of the Three Years Service Law. The Radical-Socialists and Socialists, pledged to repeal the law, made significant gains and the Socialists' vote exceeded by 300,000 their poll in 1910. Whether the Left-wing Ministry of Viviani, which took office on 16 June 1914, would have endeavoured to repeal the Three Years Law is very doubtful; the opposition of the Army, the Foreign Ministry, Poincaré and the French nationalists would have daunted a much stronger political leader than Viviani; indeed it is possible that a serious attempt to repeal the law would have resulted in a military coup. Izvolski, who was a shrewd judge of French politics, advised St. Petersburg that the conscription law would be safe enough in the hands of a relatively weak Left-wing Government.

The reaction against the *réveil national*, although demonstrating the pacific sentiments of the majority of Frenchmen, imposed a grave strain on the stability of the Republic and increased the threat to European peace. Jules Cambon remarked in 1914, 'Since the Dreyfus affair we have in France a militarist and nationalist party, which will not brook a *rapprochement* with Germany at any price and excites the aggressive tone of a great number of newspapers.' Baron Guillaume reported from Paris on 8 May 1914 that the French chauvinists had no fear of war – 'they declare themselves sure to win.' He said of the Three Years Law: 'It has been lightly imposed by the military party and the country cannot bear it. Before two years are up, they will have to abandon it or go to war.'[13]

The uneasy tensions in France were matched by those in Russia. The dismissal of Kokovtzov in January increased fears of

[13] Weber, *The Nationalist Revival in France 1905–1914*, p. 159.

a right-wing coup involving the suppression of the Duma. The arch-conservative newspaper *Kievlianin* commented in April 1914, 'we live on a volcano', and noted 'sharp displeasure with the present régime' among all classes of society.[14] The Minister of the Interior, Maklakov, made no secret of his sympathy with parties of the extreme right, while members of the *camarilla* surrounding the Empress were capable of any folly. The first months of the year were marked by numerous strikes and violent clashes between workmen and police. The Austrian chargé d'affaires commented on 17 July, 'if one continues to cling to such a senseless principle and keeps all safety-valves closed, it can happen that the revolutionary organization of Russia will be completed before her military one.' Russian decisions in July 1914 were certainly influenced by the critical internal situation.

However unpopular the Duma might be with the Tsar and his Court, it could hardly be accused of lack of patriotism. During recent years the enormous appropriations for military and naval expenditure had been willingly met, while during the Balkan Wars members had demonstrated a fierce hostility towards Austria. In spite of labour disputes, Russia was prosperous and a major industrial revolution was in full swing in the Ukraine. Members of the Duma sensed the growing strength of their country and rejoiced at the steady expansion of the armed forces. Since 1912 Russian foreign policy had achieved notable successes, and the welcome extended to the Tsar and Sazonov on their visit to the Rumanian port of Constanza on 14 June 1914 appeared to confirm Russia's ascendancy in the Balkans.

Xenophobia had always been latent in Russia and in 1914 it assumed an increasingly aggressive form. The settlement of the Liman von Sanders affair brought no real improvement in Russo-German relations, and German correspondents expressed alarm at the tone of the Russian newspapers. I. V. Bestuzhev says:

The anti-Austrian campaign in the Russian press in 1914 reached white heat. It was inflamed by the no less bitter campaign against Russia in Austria–Hungary ... It was thought that the internal crisis coming to a head in that country might at any moment compel Vienna to a more active policy in the Balkans or a direct move against Russia.[15]

[14] H. Rogger, 'Russia in 1914', *JCH* October 1966, pp. 95–6.
[15] I. V. Bestuzhev, 'Russian Foreign Policy February–June 1914', *JCH*, July 1966, p. 97.

These violent Press polemics were not calculated to soothe the nerves of Imperial Germany. On 11 March 1914 the *Post* asserted, 'a war, the like of which history has never seen, is approaching.' On 19 April the executive of the Pan-German League announced: 'France and Russia are preparing for the decisive struggle with Germany and Austria–Hungary and they intend to strike at the first favourable opportunity.' Colonel House, President Wilson's special emissary, reported from Berlin on 29 May 1914: 'The situation is extraordinary. It is militarism run stark mad. Unless someone acting for you can bring about a different understanding there is some day to be an awful cataclysm. . . . Whenever England consents, France and Russia will close in on Germany and Austria.'[16]

At a time when the foreign horizon was darkening rapidly, Germany was reaching the apex of her economic strength. Her coal production had increased by 800 per cent since 1871 – a rate surpassed only by the United States – while the development of German steel production was unparalleled. It rose from 0.9 million tons in 1886 to 13.6 millions in 1912, making Germany the second greatest steel producer in the world with an output surpassing the combined total of Britain, Russia and France. Steady expansion in textiles and mining was coupled with spectacular achievements in the chemical, electrical and optical industries. By 1913 the German mercantile marine exceeded 5,000,000 tons; German liners rivalled those of Britain on the Atlantic shipping routes, while a great expansion of docks and shipbuilding provided a solid basis for Germany's swelling overseas trade. Imperial Germany was always short of capital but, aided by state policy and the *Reichsbank*, her great banking institutions were able to play a role of increasing significance in European and overseas investment.

Yet there were certain disquieting features in the German economic pattern. The balance of trade was unfavourable while the share of Europe in her imports and exports declined by thirty per cent between 1880 and 1913. Tropical countries, and particularly South America, were supplying an increasing proportion of Germany's raw materials. This led some German economists to demand an expansion of the European basis of

[16] C. Seymour, *The Intimate Papers of Colonel House* (Boston, 1926), I, p. 249. House's words are often quoted but usually without the reference to France and Russia.

German power. Associations were formed which pressed for a close economic union with Austria–Hungary, and for the incorporation of other countries in a new *Zollverein*. Max Schinkel, director of Germany's second largest bank, the *Disconto-Gesellschaft*, declared that a broader basis was required 'for laying the economic foundations of German world policy'.[17] Between 1912 and 1914 the famous Walther Rathenau, the leading figure in *Allgemeine-Elektrizitätsgesellschaft*, pressed on Bethmann Hollweg the need for a central European customs union and foreshadowed the conception of *Mitteleuropa* which was to assume such importance during the war.

The deductions drawn from these developments by members of the Fischer school are disarming in their simplicity. Geiss says: 'German *Weltpolitik*, the containment policy of the Entente and Germany's refusal to be contained made war inevitable.'[18] Yet many German magnates like Albert Ballin, General Director of the Hamburg-America Company, were ardent advocates of peace. So far from wishing to rush into war, these industrialists appreciated that, if Germany could postpone a conflict, the advantages would be all in her favour. German capitalists were gaining a significant place in the French steel industry, and had a controlling interest in many of the new enterprises in the Ukraine. Taylor says: 'The great capitalists were winning the mastery of Europe without war; the industries of southern Russia, the iron-fields of Lorraine and Normandy were already largely under their control.' In 1913 Hugo Stinnes, the great Ruhr industrialist, told Class, the President of the Pan-German League: 'Give us three or four more years of peace and Germany will be the unchallenged economic master of Europe.' Yet German capitalists might have been wise to refrain from building up great enterprises in France or Russia; in particular German investment in the Ukraine was contributing significantly to Russia's military revival.

German foreign policy in 1914 failed to pursue a definite course. Her vacillations over Turkey have already been noted, while her attitude to the Balkans was ambivalent. It was in vain that Berchtold urged the need for an agreement with Bulgaria, combined with a Turco-Bulgarian entente. In May 1914 Wangenheim, the German ambassador in Constantinople, considered that if

[17] Fischer, *Germany's Aims in the First World War*, p. 10.
[18] Geiss, *July 1914*, p. 35.

only Berlin and Vienna would see eye to eye on Balkan matters, a Turco-Bulgarian treaty could be concluded overnight. But the Kaiser's dislike of Ferdinand was matched by his obsession with the Greek Royal family. Helmreich says: 'Jagow, following the Kaiser's instructions, had from the very beginning of the negotiations done his best to sabotage the Turco-Bulgarian entente and replace it by a Turco-Greek one.'[19] With great difficulty Berchtold persuaded Berlin to float a loan for a desperate Bulgaria in June 1914, but hope of an Austro-Bulgarian alliance was wrecked by the contemptuous attitude of the Kaiser coupled with that of the Archduke Franz Ferdinand.

Nor did Germany and Austria achieve anything in their dealings with Rumania. In December 1913 King Carol told Count Czernin, the Austrian minister, that the treatment of Rumanians in Hungary was a fatal obstacle to good relations, and Czernin concluded that 'the treaty of alliance is not worth the ink and paper on which it is written.' The sensible course would have been to throw Rumania overboard and concentrate all efforts on winning Bulgaria but, when the Kaiser visited Vienna in March 1914, he fully agreed with Count Tisza, the Hungarian Prime Minister, that it was of the utmost importance to keep Rumania in the Triple Alliance. However, the Kaiser was so ill-informed about Balkan affairs that he described Tisza, the arch-oppressor of the Rumanians, as 'a really great statesman' and 'a quite outstanding man of firm will and clear ideas.' Meanwhile the Russo-Rumanian *rapprochement* developed apace and, as Czernin said, German policy revealed 'the most incredible short-sightedness that ever was.' So much for Fischer's assertion that by the summer of 1914 the war had been 'well prepared diplomatically'.[20]

In the spring of 1914 rumours circulated that Serbia and Montenegro were preparing some treaty of union and, when Pasich saw the Tsar on 2 February, Nicholas expressed strong approval of the proposal. Berchtold regarded this development with deep concern, but the Kaiser commented on 11 March 1914: 'This union is definitely not to be prevented, and if Vienna were to attempt this, it would be committing a great stupidity and conjuring up the danger of a war with the Slavs, which would leave

[19] Helmreich, p. 413.

[20] Fischer, 'Deutschlands Schuld am Ausbruch des Ersten Weltkriegs', *Die Zeit*, 3 September 1965, p. 30.

us quite cold.' There seems to be no justification for Fischer's contention that frustrated economic ambitions in south-eastern Europe were driving Germany into war.[21]

In her dealings with Britain, Germany did somewhat better and, as we have seen, by June 1914 she was ready to sign agreements with her about the Bagdad railway and the Portuguese colonies. Bethmann Hollweg had some hope that he was about to achieve an understanding with Britain which might guarantee her neutrality; moreover, the very serious troubles which developed in Ireland in 1914 and the violent and irresponsible support given by some Conservative politicians to the Ulster Orangemen seemed to threaten Britain with civil war.

However, Bethmann's confidence in British intentions received a sharp setback in May 1914 when the Germans learned, through a spy in the Russian embassy in London, that Britain and Russia were entering into secret naval negotiations. On 21 April King George V and Grey had visited Paris and, at Russian instigation, Doumergue, the Foreign Minister, had urged Grey to yield to Russia's request for a naval convention. The Russian Admiralty attached considerable importance to such an agreement and a conference at St. Petersburg on 26 May decided: 'If England could hold the larger part of the German Fleet in the North Sea, a Russian landing in Pomerania might be attempted, though British transports, despatched before the opening of hostilities, would be essential.' In fact the Russian proposals were quite unrealistic. Russia had laid down four dreadnought battleships for her Baltic Fleet in 1912 and was intending to build another four dreadnoughts in the period 1914–17. The British naval attaché to Russia reported on 19 March 1914 that his German counterpart had also recognized 'the fundamental mistake of the Russian Admiralty in devoting its energy and money principally to an increase of purely material strength rather than to the far more urgent problem of building up a system of honest administration and the creation of a well-trained, capable, well-paid and contented personnel.'[22]

The British Cabinet agreed to naval negotiations with Russia in May 1914, but early in June the Wilhelmstrasse arranged for

[21] Fischer, 'Weltpolitik, Weltmachtstreben und deutsche Kriegsziele', *HZ*, 199, 1964.

[22] Marder, *From the Dreadnought to Scapa Flow*, I, p. 310. However the Russians led the rest of the world in naval mines.

the *Berliner Tageblatt* to reveal the story. Challenged about this in the House of Commons on 11 June, Grey replied that 'no such negotiations are in progress and none are likely to be entered upon as far as I can judge.' Gooch remarks that this was 'the only occasion on which he deliberately misled his countrymen.' Disturbed by the public clamour, Grey decided to postpone the conclusion of a naval agreement until the visit of Prince Louis of Battenberg, the First Sea Lord, to Russia in August.

This incident is not without importance but its significance has been much exaggerated by Egmont Zechlin, Fischer's colleague at the University of Hamburg. According to him these secret Anglo-Russian talks and Grey's prevarications created a 'crisis of trust' between Britain and Germany and drove Bethmann Hollweg into the desperate gamble of backing Austria in July 1914.[23] This far-fetched argument is rightly repudiated by Fischer, although he distorts the facts by asserting that Germany could have prevented further negotiations and by his claim that Grey's postponement of the talks constituted a step towards Germany.[24]

John Moses remarks that in the summer of 1914 'according to Fischer, Germany was not merely in a posture of war like all the other powers, but was rather on the prowl awaiting a favourable moment to strike like a beast of prey.'[25] While there were very dangerous forces at work in Germany in 1914, it is hard to see the Kaiser or Bethmann Hollweg as ruthless militarists eager to assert Germany's claim to world power. The idea of preventive war was certainly gaining ground in Germany in 1914, and Bethmann's reflections, recorded in the diary of his confidential secretary, Kurt Riezler, reveal a deep pessimism about the international situation. On 5 June Bassermann, the Conservative politician, wrote: '. . . Bethmann said to me with fatalistic resignation: "If there is war with France, England will march against us to the last man".' Riezler's diary records similar pessimism and W. J. Mommsen remarks:

. . . however Riezler's diary is interpreted, one thing is incontrovertible, namely the alarming spirit of fatalism in which wide circles of the German

[23] E. Zechlin, 'Deutschland zwischen Kabinetts-und Wirtschaftskrieg', *HZ* 199, 1964.

[24] Fischer, *Weltmacht oder Niedergang*, pp. 55–7.

[25] J. Moses, *The War Aims of Imperial Germany: Professor Fritz Fischer and his Critics* (University of Queensland, 1968), p. 217.

(and indeed not only the German) public, as well as their political leaders, awaited the approaching war. This was a frame of mind that, when the hour of crisis came, decisively weakened the will to preserve peace.[26]

Fischer's thesis hinges on his basic assumption that Germany reckoned on being able to deal militarily with Russia and France; in fact the German General Staff was far from confident about the balance of forces. On 12 May 1914 Moltke and Conrad met for staff discussions at Carlsbad in Bohemia. According to Conrad, Moltke confirmed that he would stake everything on the Schlieffen Plan but expressed doubts of its success, saying, 'I'll do what I can. We are not superior to the French.' For Moltke, time was running out for the Central Powers; he had no great confidence in victory in 1914 but thought that the situation could only get worse. Moltke told Conrad that 'delay meant a lessening of our chances; we could not compete with Russia in masses.'

Moltke's pessimism is confirmed from other sources. In a memorandum drawn up in 1913, he had reckoned that once the enemies of Germany and Austria had mobilized their forces, they would have a superiority of twelve army corps. He was profoundly impressed by the reorganization of the Russian Army and the French adoption of three years military service; this implied a steady worsening of Germany's position. If Bethmann Hollweg still retained some illusions about British intervention in a European war, Moltke regarded it as certain. As for the Austrians, Moltke predicted that 'Austria–Hungary's offensive capability would not last long.' Corelli Barnett comments: 'Thus the German plan of campaign was not at all an aggression plotted by a general staff conscious of great power, but a desperate sally by men haunted by numerical weakness.'[27]

With regard to the German Naval Staff, P. H. S. Hatton writes:

The German Embassy myth – which London accepted – in 1914 as in 1911–12, of Tirpitz as the leader of the war party, is in the process of being exploded. Tirpitz did not desire war, although he was not above using war scares in order to justify his naval building programme. In his

[26] W. J. Mommsen, 'The Debate on German War Aims', *JCH*, July 1966, p. 63. Portions of Riezler's diary were first published by K. D. Erdmann, 'Zur Beurteilung Bethmann Hollwegs', *Geschichte in Wissenschaft und Unterricht*, XV 1964.

[27] C. Barnett, *The Swordbearers: Studies in Supreme Command in the First World War* (London, 1963), p. 31.

own memoirs he claimed to have been against war in 1914, and Ritter has demonstrated that Tirpitz in the July crisis was in favour of a diplomatic solution and withdrew from earlier militant positions. Tirpitz did not desire to send his fleet to almost certain destruction nor to see it grow unseaworthy by being blockaded in harbour.[28]

Britain's naval preponderance over Germany in 1914 was very substantial. She had twenty dreadnought battleships to Germany's thirteen, nine battle-cruisers to Germany's six, and twenty-six pre-dreadnought battleships to Germany's twelve. Her superiority in cruisers, although not in destroyers or submarines, was more than two to one. The opening of the Kiel Canal to dreadnought battleships in June 1914 was of strategic importance to Germany but, even allowing for the high quality of German gunnery, seamanship and naval construction, Tirpitz knew well that the High Seas Fleet had no hope of coping with the Royal Navy in a major battle.

British naval superiority was a factor making for peace, but the prodigious development of Russian armaments threatened to alter the whole balance of European power. This most ominous of all elements threatening European peace was aggravated by Sukhomlinov's practice of inspiring newspaper articles proclaiming the tremendous growth of the Russian Army. Annotating a despatch from St. Petersburg, dated 11 March 1914, the Kaiser wrote: 'I . . . do not entertain the slightest doubt that Russia is systematically preparing war against us and I shall govern my policy accordingly.' After reading a particularly provocative Russian article in June, Wilhelm commented: 'Well! At last the Russians have shown their hand! Anyone in Germany who still believes that Russia-Gaul is not working at high pressure for an early war against us and that we must not take corresponding counter-measures, deserves to be sent straight to the Dalldorf lunatic asylum.' On 18 July 1914 Jagow wrote to the German ambassador in London: 'In a few years according to all expert opinion, Russia will be ready to strike. Then she will crush us with the numbers of her soldiers; then she will have built her Baltic Fleet and strategic railways. Our group meanwhile will be growing steadily weaker.'

Recent examination of Jagow's private papers has shown that 'in May or early June 1914' Moltke told the Foreign Secretary

[28] P. H. S. Hatton, 'Britain and Germany in 1914. The July Crisis and War Aims, *PP*, April 1967. p. 142.

that in view of Russia's growing armaments there was no alternative but to 'wage a preventive war in order to beat the enemy
while we still have some chance of winning'. Whether this remark,
made in a motor car travelling between Potsdam and Berlin,
deserves the great significance attached to it by Geiss may well
be doubted but, in any case, Jagow disagreed, pointing to 'the
steady improvement of Germany's economic situation.' Similarly
Bethmann Hollweg, in conversation with the Bavarian minister
in Berlin, Count Lerchenfeld, in June 1914, admitted that many
generals were demanding a preventive war, but said that he
thought the moment for it had passed. Lerchenfeld quotes the
Chancellor as saying:

> There are circles in the Reich who expect of a war an improvement in
> the domestic situation in Germany – in a Conservative direction. He, the
> Chancellor, however, thought that on the contrary a World War with its
> incalculable consequences would strengthen tremendously the power of
> Social Democracy, because they preached peace, and would topple
> many a throne.[29]

In one sense, however, Germany was guilty of aggravating to
a grave degree the perilous situation of Europe. All military
thinking in Europe was dominated by the implications of the
Schlieffen Plan. The French and Russian staffs were well aware
of its general character, and their own plans were aimed at
dislocating it by violent offensives of their own. Joffre and his
'Young Turks' were convinced that they could win a great battle
in Lorraine and cut off a German circling move through Belgium
by a series of devastating blows in Luxemburg and the Ardennes.
In the 75 mm. gun, the French believed that they had the best
field artillery in the world and the excellence of the German field
howitzer was to be a cruel surprise to them. Both the Germans
and the French underrated the machine-gun, but the Germans
were better prepared to exploit this weapon. The French High
Command miscalculated the German strength; although they
reckoned with German reserve formations in the opening battles,
they never believed that as many as thirteen reserve corps would
be committed to the initial thrust. By utilizing her own reserve
formations, France could have outnumbered the Germans from
the start but, in the view of the French General Staff, *'les réserves,
c'est zéro.'* On mobilization the French were prepared to incor-

[29] Geiss, *July 1914*, p. 47.

porate reservists in the existing formations of the standing army, but they shrank from the dangerous heresy of throwing reserve divisions or corps into front-line battle.

The Franco-Russian General Staff Conference held at St. Petersburg in August 1913 confirmed the opinion expressed at the conferences of 1910, 1911, and 1912 that 'Germany will direct the greatest part of her forces against France, and leave only a minimum of troops against Russia.' The Conference declared that it was 'essential that the French armies are able to have a marked superiority over the German forces in the west' – hence Russia must launch a major offensive against Germany as soon as possible after the fifteenth day of mobilization. In conversations with General Joffre in 1912 and 1913 the Tsar's formidable uncle, the Grand Duke Nicholas, gave categorical assurances that Russia would invade East Prussia as rapidly as possible. Historians of 1914 have not attached adequate weight to these assurances, and have failed to appreciate how the potential application of the Schlieffen Plan would automatically entail intense activity in eastern Europe. Russia would have to mobilize rapidly and invade Germany to relieve pressure on France, while Austria would have to launch a massive invasion of southern Poland to tie down the principal Russian forces and prevent them destroying the German Eighth Army in East Prussia. The urgent need of both France and Germany for rapid mobilization and early offensive action by their eastern allies accelerated the whole tempo of the crisis of July 1914.

CHAPTER FIVE

Sarajevo and the Ultimatum, 28 June–23 July 1914

IN June 1914 the British Admiralty accepted an invitation to send four battle-cruisers to the Russian harbour of Kronstadt and four battleships to attend the ceremonies at Kiel to mark the re-opening of the canal. The decision to permit eight of Britain's precious dreadnoughts to sail into the Baltic was one of the most irresponsible ever taken by a British government; since Agadir a considerable portion of the Royal Navy had been kept at constant readiness and much attention had been devoted to the possibility of a 'bolt from the blue' attack similar to the one launched by the Japanese at Port Arthur. Yet for several days four dreadnought battleships of the *King George V* class lay at Kiel, anchored in the midst of the German Navy and dependent for their security on the Kaiser's good faith and sense of hospitality. Churchill says of the Kiel visit:

Officers and men fraternized and entertained each other afloat and ashore. Together they strolled arm in arm through the hospitable town, or dined with all goodwill in mess and wardroom. . . . In the midst of these festivities, on the 28th June, arrived the news of the murder of the Archduke . . . at Sarajevo. The Emperor was out sailing when he received it. He came on shore in noticeable agitation, and that same evening, cancelling his other arrangements, quitted Kiel.[1]

The full story of the Sarajevo assassination has yet to be told and, in spite of much learned research, many vital points remain obscure. Whether the details of the assassination merit the torrents of ink expended on them by historians may well be doubted. Sarajevo provided the spark which started the Great War but, in view of the inflammable state of Europe in 1914, a major international crisis could hardly have been postponed for very much longer. This need not necessarily have led to war – any more than Sarajevo – but it seems highly probable that a 'showdown' was impending among the Great Powers.

[1] W. S. Churchill, *The World Crisis 1911–1914*, pp. 187–8.

The removal of the Archduke Franz Ferdinand from the European scene was an event of considerable importance, quite apart from the circumstances of his death. He was an unattractive personality, sullen, suspicious and addicted to blood sports but, apart from a deep hatred of Italy, he was an influence for peace. Norman Stone says: 'The assassination of Francis Ferdinand was not only the occasion for the outbreak of the First World War, it was also a prime cause, with his removal nothing shielded Berchtold from Conrad's bellicose demands.'[2] Whether Conrad was particularly bellicose in the summer of 1914 is rather questionable; his own memoranda show that he then believed that the odds were heavily against Austria, although Ritter quotes him as saying that 'so ancient a Monarchy and so glorious an Army' ought not to perish without putting up a fight.[3]

The murder of the Archduke is frequently attributed to his alleged desire to establish 'trialism' and frustrate Serbian national ambitions by granting concessions to the South Slavs. Dedijer throws considerable doubt on whether these were really Franz Ferdinand's intentions and, in any case, many Serb nationalists and Bosnian Slavs regarded him as their worst enemy and thought he was working for a war with Russia and Serbia. In spite of all efforts by historians the motives for the assassination remain obscure. It may be regarded merely as a violent expression of South Slav patriotism, or it can be interpreted as a deliberate provocation intended to lure Austria into the course of action which she actually pursued. The fact that the murder was planned and organized by Colonel Dimitrievich, Chief of the Intelligence Section of the Serbian General Staff and head of the terrorist society known as the 'Black Hand', lends some support to the latter view.

In March 1914 Austrian newspapers announced that Franz Ferdinand and his wife would visit Sarajevo, capital of Bosnia, on 28 June – a solemn day for the Serbs because it was the anniversary of the defeat at Kossovo in 1389 which terminated their independence. Dimitrievich arranged for a youth named Princip and two fellow terrorists from Bosnia to receive training in Belgrade in revolver-shooting and bomb-throwing; he provided

[2] N. Stone, 'Conrad von Hötzendorf, Austrian Chief of Staff', *History Today*, July 1963, p. 484.
[3] Ritter, 'Der Anteil der Militärs an der Kriegskatastrophe von 1914', *HZ*, 1961, 193, p. 83.

them with arms, saw that they were briefed on their role, and arranged for frontier guards to facilitate their crossing into Bosnia. On the late morning of 28 June Princip duly shot the Archduke and his consort in Sarajevo, although his task was certainly made easier by the incompetent police arrangements of General Potiorek, the Governor of Bosnia.

There is no doubt that the Serbian Prime Minister, Pasich, and Dimitrievich's military superior, Marshal Putnik, were aware of the plot. The 'Black Hand' was hostile to the Radical Government of Pasich; the Prime Minister told the Cabinet of the conspiracy but attempted to prevent it and sent a vague warning to the Austrian Government. He may have intended his warning to be more specific, and it is possible that his instructions were deliberately bungled by Jovanovich, the Serbian minister in Vienna.[4] Dimitrievich is said to have tried to restrain Princip and his associates at the last moment, but the evidence is far from conclusive. Geiss argues from this that 'in the last analysis, the murder at Sarajevo was thus primarily the deed of Princip himself and can only indirectly be charged to the "Black Hand", and virtually not at all to the Serbian Government. . . .'[5] Whatever may be thought of this argument, it runs counter to an accepted principle of international law that a government is responsible for acts of violence which emanate from its territory.

Pasich was expecting very serious trouble in 1914. On 2 February he appealed to Russia to provide arms 'before next spring' because of the threat to the status quo posed by Austria, Bulgaria and Turkey. The Tsar's Government was entreated to furnish weapons and munitions, clothing for 250,000 soldiers, telegraphs, telephones and four wireless stations. Sazonov asked Sukhomlinov to help but on 30 March the latter declined because of the needs of the Russian Army; shortly afterwards Sazonov told the Serbs that about half the requirements could be met. Gooch says: 'At the opening of June the impatience of Pasich for Russian munitions became almost feverish, both Hartwig and Sazonov supporting his request.'[6] On 30 June, two days after the murder, the acting Chief of the Russian

---

[4] According to Albertini, II, p. 106, Jovanovich was designated by the 'Black Hand' to be Foreign Minister in the Government intended to replace that of Pasich. Albertini describes him as 'a frenzied Serb nationalist'.

[5] Geiss, *July 1914*, pp. 52–3.

[6] Gooch, p. 175, interpreting Russian diplomatic documents.

General Staff passed on the Tsar's approval of Pasich's request for munitions, while on the same day Sazonov sent a 'very secret and urgent' letter to the Navy Minister asking for a report on the state of the Black Sea Fleet.

Albertini says that 'it does . . . seem certain' that Colonel Artamonov, the Russian military attaché in Belgrade, 'was told of the plot, if not directly by Dimitriević, then by some other informant, and that he did nothing to thwart it'.[7] At his trial for treason at Salonika in April 1917, Dimitrievich admitted planning the Archduke's murder, but denied collaborating with Artamonov in the plot. His denial means little as he dared not antagonize the Russian Government which later made vain efforts for his reprieve. Moreover, it is hard to believe that Hartwig, the rabid Austrophobe and the constant guide and mentor of the Serbian Government, was not consulted by Pasich and did not have detailed knowledge of what was afoot. After the murder, Hartwig reported to St. Petersburg that 'all Serbia expressed sympathy and strongly condemned the crime of the two madmen'. This tongue-in-cheek statement is the last evidence we have from Hartwig; he dropped dead while visiting the Austrian legation in Belgrade on 10 July.

The evidence of Plamenatz, the Foreign Minister of Montenegro, deserves consideration. In April 1914 he learned that Russia would renew the subsidy to Montenegro, pay arrears, and provide food and clothing for 50,000 men. King Nicholas, two of whose daughters were married to Russian Grand Dukes, was told that war with Austria was 'not far off'. The Serbian minister at Cetinje remarked to Plamenatz after Sarajevo, 'this cartridge will bring liberty to the whole Serb race.' He added that Serbia was sure of Russian support.[8]

Franz Ferdinand was very unpopular at court where there was little mourning for the victims of Sarajevo. The Emperor Franz Josef had never forgiven his nephew for his morganatic marriage and commented on hearing of the outrage, 'horrible, but the Almighty does not allow Himself to be flouted with impunity.' Nevertheless there was a general impression in Austrian Government circles that vigorous action would be necessary against Serbia in order to prevent the Monarchy from disintegrating. Albertini says: 'All diplomatic reports to foreign governments

[7] Albertini, II, p. 86. He is sceptical of Artamonov's denial in 1937.
[8] Gooch, p. 217. See note on Captain Werchovski in Albertini II p.86 *n*.

agree on this.' When Conrad told his staff on 29 June that 'the outrage was a Serbian machination, which had created an extremely serious situation and would lead to war with Serbia', he was voicing an opinion held by nearly all responsible statesmen and officials in the Monarchy, with the exception of Count Tisza. On 29 June, the Foreign Minister informed Tisza 'of his intention to make the Sarajevo outrage an occasion for a settlement of accounts with Serbia'. Nevertheless on the same day Berchtold rejected Conrad's demand for immediate mobilization against Serbia and stressed the need for an enquiry which 'may furnish us with a reason for taking action', together with the need for prior consultation with Germany.

Berchtold has fared badly at the hands of most historians who tend to represent him as a shallow dilettante, sadly lacking in intelligence or will power. However, Norman Stone comments that 'Berchtold's despatches from St. Petersburg show him as a man of great perception', while Gooch says: 'He had made an excellent ambassador at St. Petersburg ... and his despatches are from the literary point of view among the best of his time.' He was certainly not a strong character but he was very far from being the weak, vacillating creature he has been pictured.

On 1 July Count Hoyos, Berchtold's *chef de cabinet*, received a call from the influential German publicist, Victor Naumann, who was in close touch with the Wilhelmstrasse. Naumann stressed the great uneasiness felt in Berlin about Russian armaments and said that 'the idea of a preventive war with Russia was viewed with less disfavour than a year ago.' It was believed that England would remain neutral and that France would restrain Russia but, if it came to war, the Triple Alliance was strong enough. Naumann said that, 'In his opinion ... it was a question of life and death for the Monarchy not to leave this crime unpunished but to annihilate Serbia.'

On 4 July Hoyos was despatched to Berlin with a diplomatic memorandum and an autograph letter to the Kaiser from Franz Josef. Albertini remarks: 'If the word "war" does not appear in either document, there are expressions which amount to the same thing. What is meant by "with a firm hand to sever the threads which its enemies sought to draw closer into a net ..." and by "eliminate Serbia as a power factor in the Balkans" unless it be that she was to be attacked and annihilated?'[9] On 5 July the

[9] Albertini, II, p. 134.

Kaiser considered these messages in a conversation with the Austrian ambassador, Count Szögyeny, at Potsdam.

The news of the murder of the Archduke, a close personal friend, had a shattering effect on the Kaiser; he commented, 'now or never' on a despatch from Tschirschky, dated 30 June, reporting a desire in Vienna for 'a thorough settlement of accounts with the Serbs', and expressed great anger at a statement by the ambassador that he had uttered a warning against hasty measures. Geiss brings out the very important point that the Kaiser had secret conferences with Bethmann Hollweg on 1 and 3 July;[10] obviously they considered the situation created by the assassination and decided on a line of policy. It is quite wrong to state, as many historians have done, that in giving a 'blank cheque' to Austria the Kaiser was acting on his own initiative; it is equally incorrect to say, as Craig does, that 'a Crown Council' was held to decide on German action.

The upshot of the famous luncheon at Potsdam was that the Kaiser urged Austria–Hungary to make war on Serbia; on the return of Hoyos to Vienna on 7 July, Berchtold was able to assure Conrad: 'Germany advises us to strike at once. ... Germany will support us unreservedly even if our march into Serbia lets loose the great war.' When the Kaiser saw Bethmann Hollweg on the evening of 5 July, the Chancellor raised no objection to this policy and indeed backed it to the hilt. Incidentally Moltke had nothing to do with these decisions. On 28 June he had arrived at Carlsbad for a 'cure' and remained there until the evening of 25 July.

On the evening of 5 July the Kaiser conferred with General von Falkenhayn, the Prussian Minister of War. To a direct question from the Kaiser whether the Army was ready for all contingencies, Falkenhayn replied briefly and unconditionally that it was 'ready'. According to his biographer, General von Zwehl, the Minister urged the Kaiser 'to prepare for war', but this the Kaiser refused to do 'for fear of interfering with the action of diplomacy'.[11] After the interview Falkenhayn wrote to Moltke in curiously reassuring terms and advised him to continue his 'cure' at Carlsbad. On the morning of the 6th the Kaiser saw General Bertrab, the senior General Staff officer in Berlin, who telegraphed to Moltke as follows:

[10] Geiss, *July 1914*, p. 61.
[11] H. von Zwehl, *Erich von Falkenhayn* (Berlin, 1926), p. 55.

. . . the Emperor of Austria–Hungary has resolved to march into Serbia. His Majesty in agreement with the Foreign Ministry and War Ministry approves this decision and has expressed his readiness to cover Austria in the event of Russia's intervening. It is true His Majesty does not think that Russia will intervene; particularly in view of the cause, the Tsar of Russia will hardly decide to do so. His Majesty therefore regards the affair as in the first instance a purely Balkan concern and signifies this conception by departing on his northern cruise according to plan.[12]

On the advice of Bethmann Hollweg, the Kaiser left for Kiel on the morning of 6 July. There he consulted with Baron Krupp, who sent an urgent enquiry to his board of directors asking 'whether anything should be done to supplement the firm's stocks in case of mobilization'. They were reported to be adequate, even in the event of a blockade, but it may well be asked why the Kaiser or Bethmann Hollweg did not consult with other industrialists, who could have informed them of the fearful inadequacy of Germany's resources in many vital raw materials. If Germany intended to risk a major conflict – and Bethmann told Riezler on 6 July that 'an action against Serbia can lead to a world war' – then common-sense demanded that no irrevocable step should be taken until adequate reserves had been accumulated in rubber, oil, corn and cotton, to say nothing of copper, manganese, tin and mercury. Prince von Bülow comments:

. . . the very worst of all the errors of those . . . individuals who led their country to disaster was that of having taken such grave decisions . . . without once consulting a diplomat of experience, or any intelligent business man informed on international economics. Albert Ballin, Arthur Gwinner, Emil Rathenau, Max Warburg, Karl Fürstenberg, Paul von Schwabach, might all have been asked. In the second year of war Albert Ballin said to me with a sigh: 'Had I known the intentions of Bethmann Hollweg and Jagow in the summer of 1914 – had I even been given the barest hint of the terms of the proposed ultimatum to Serbia, I could at least have taken an off chance and got food supplies into Germany in time.'[13]

The Kaiser told Krupp that he would declare war immediately if Russia mobilized; Krupp recorded: 'The Emperor's repeated

---

[12] Albertini, II, p. 142, quoting A. Bach, *Deutsche Gesandtschaftsberichte zum Kriegsausbruch 1914* (Berlin, 1937), p. 14. Bertrab, the Chief of the Cartographic Section of the General Staff, was not a significant figure and merely acted as a messenger.

[13] Bülow, *Memoirs 1909–1919*, p. 173.

insistence that in this matter no one would be able to reproach him again with want of resolution produced an almost comic effect.' On 7 July the *Hohenzollern* departed for Norwegian waters, where the Kaiser continued to cruise for nearly three weeks.

The Kaiser and Bethmann Hollweg were courting a great war because they seem to have thought that, unless Austria took vigorous action against the South Slav movement, she was doomed as a Great Power and would be useless as an ally. Geiss argues that they had wider views:

> From what Riezler recorded in his now famous diary, it appears that the Chancellor was not only fully aware of the possible consequences when taking his 'leap into the dark' – war with Britain, i.e. world war – but that already at that stage his first objective seems to have been war with Russia and France; a diplomatic victory – France dropping Russia, Russia dropping Serbia – would have been accepted only as a second best.[14]

However, the view that Bethmann deliberately intended to force war on Russia and France can hardly be sustained. The fact that Germany made no serious military or economic preparations for war between 6 and 23 July indicates that, at this stage, the Chancellor hoped to localize an Austro-Serbian conflict. This is confirmed by the letter from Jagow to Lichnowsky, the ambassador in London, on 18 July:

> We must attempt to localize the conflict between Austria and Serbia. Whether this is possible will depend in the first place on Russia and in the second place on the moderating influence of the other members of the Entente. The more boldness Austria displays the more strongly we support her, the more likely is Russia to keep quiet. There is certain to be some blustering in St. Petersburg, but at bottom Russia is not now ready to strike. Nor will France and England be anxious for war at the present time.

However, too much importance should not be attached to this wish to localize an Austro-Serbian war. If Germany and Austria had been able to crush Serbia their military position would have been very significantly improved, but for this reason the prospects of their being permitted to do so were exceedingly slight. As

[14] Geiss, 'The Outbreak of the First World War and German War Aims', *JCH*, July 1966, p. 83. Geiss does not appreciate that 'Russia dropping Serbia', so far from being a mere diplomatic victory, would have profoundly altered the military balance in Europe.

Prince von Bülow says, Bethmann Hollweg and Jagow constituted a 'committee for public catastrophe'.

Before the presentation of the ultimatum, there was no high-level discussion among German Army leaders. Moltke's deputy, General Waldersee, questioned by the Reichstag Commission after the war, declared 'there was nothing to initiate . . . the Army was, as always, ready.' On 17 July Waldersee wrote to Jagow, 'I shall remain here, [in Berlin] ready to jump; we are all prepared at the General Staff; in the meantime there is nothing to do.' From this one would gather that the General Staff was anticipating a European war. Yet there is strong reason to doubt whether this was the case. Falkenhayn was sceptical of Austria's warlike intentions while on 7 July Lieut.-Colonel Kageneck, the German military attaché in Vienna, reported to Moltke that it looked as if war with Serbia was a certainty. When he gave a similar warning on 13 July Moltke commented: 'Austria must beat the Serbs and then make peace quickly, demanding an Austro-Serbian alliance as the sole condition. Like Prussia did with Austria in 1866.'[15] The enigmatic Chief of Staff thought it unnecessary to return to Berlin.

Tirpitz was away on holiday in Switzerland but Admiral von Capelle, who had been briefed by the Kaiser on 6 July, called a secret Admiralty conference which decided to hasten the construction of all nearly-completed small craft; to augment the fuel supplies; to provide fleet auxiliaries and store ships; 'to put into shape' the naval flying service; and to send a battleship on a test trip through the recently deepened Kiel canal. The battle-cruiser *Goeben* was ordered to Pola for repairs to her boiler tubes, while Admiral von Spee, commander in the Pacific, was told on 10 July that war between Austria and Serbia was possible and England might be involved if it came to a general war. He was ordered to remain at Ponape in the Carolines 'in certain and constant communication'.

The Navy seems to have been the only organization in Germany which was making a serious effort to get ready for war. No doubt, as Waldersee indicated to Jagow on 17 July, the Army's mobilization machine was ready to go into action at the push of a button, but many technical measures could have been taken to increase the readiness of the arms and services or the tempo

[15] Albertini, II, p. 154, quoting Bach, pp. 15–16.

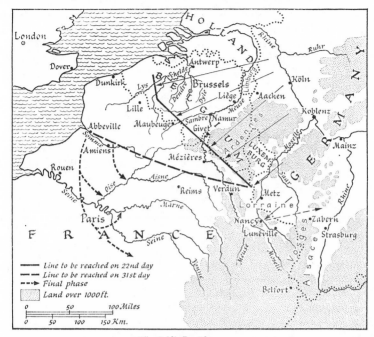

The Schlieffen Plan, 1905

of preparation in frontier zones. It is clear from the Kaiser's remark to Falkenhayn on 5 July that he declined to countenance such measures because they might prejudice the prospects of localizing an Austro-Serbian war.

Germany had cleared the ground for Austrian action, but the Government in Vienna was slow to respond. Taylor says that 'Berchtold dawdled in typical Viennese fashion'; but he had serious difficulties to overcome. At the Imperial Council on 7 July, Tisza admitted that Austria was entitled to formulate stiff demands on Serbia and send an ultimatum if she refused to accept them, but he would 'never agree to a surprise attack on Serbia without preliminary diplomatic preparation' or to her annihilation as an independent state. He said that 'it does not lie with Germany to judge whether or not we should now strike at Serbia.' The Austrian Prime Minister, Count Stürgkh, said the situation 'decidedly calls for a solution at the point of the sword', but

Tisza still refused to accept the despatch of an ultimatum so harsh that Serbia would be almost certain to reject it.

On 13 July Berchtold was informed by Dr. Wiesner, the Legal Counsellor at the Ballplatz whom he had sent to Sarajevo, that 'there is nothing to show the complicity of the Serbian Government in directing the assassination or in its preparations.' Wiesner even declared that this was 'altogether out of the question'. He did say, however, that Serbian officials had provided arms and smuggled the assassins across the frontier and that the Serbian propaganda organization *Narodna Obrana* might be involved. On 14 July Berchtold finally succeeded in persuading Tisza to consent to the despatch of a very severe ultimatum, on condition that only slight frontier rectifications would be demanded in case of war. The Hungarian Prime Minister is said to have yielded because of the violent and unrepentant tone of the Serbian Press.

The ultimatum was deliberately framed in terms which no self-respecting state could accept. Serbia was required to suppress all propaganda directed against the Monarchy, to dissolve *Narodna Obrana*, to remove from the Army and administration such persons as the Austrian Government might stipulate, to arrest certain individuals, to punish severely frontier officials involved in illegal activity, and most important 'to accept the collaboration in Serbia of representatives of the Austro-Hungarian Government for the suppression of the subversive movement directed against the territorial integrity of the Monarchy.' Berchtold decided to postpone its presentation until Poincaré and Viviani had concluded the visit which they were due to pay to Russia between 20 and 23 July. In spite of the recent renewal of the Triple Alliance in December 1912 and friendly assurances by General Pollio, the Italian Chief of Staff, both the German and Austrian Governments carefully refrained from consulting Italy. Despite all precautions, nervousness spread in Germany and Austria and after 12 July there were heavy falls on the Berlin and Vienna Stock Exchanges.

The arrival of Poincaré and Viviani in Russia was preceded by triumphant fanfares in Paris proclaiming the strength of the Triple Entente. Great stress was laid in the Paris newspapers on the effect of the 'enormous masses of the Russian Army on the balance of power'. The correspondent of *Le Matin* reported on 18 July: 'M. Poincaré arrives at the moment when this country is becoming the strongest military power and when it is on the eve of becoming the leading nation from the agricultural, industrial and commercial points of view.' The Left-wing *Bataille Syndicaliste* commented on 19 July: 'In truth one has the impression on reading *Le Temps* and *Le Matin* that our patriots do not merely foresee a possible war but that they envisage a prompt conflict.' Taking its tone from Paris, the *Lyon Républicain* declared on 24 July that with its control of the seas and inexhaustible manpower, 'the Triple Entente holds the destinies of Europe in its hands.'[16]

At St. Petersburg Poincaré met his close friend, Maurice de Paléologue, former Political Director at the Quai d'Orsay, whose appointment as ambassador to Russia he had specially arranged. A man of brilliant intellect and great persuasive powers, an ardent patriot who longed to restore the 'glories of France', Paléologue fully represented the *réveil national* and the aggressive confidence of the French General Staff. According to Paléologue, the Prime Minister, Doumergue, said to him before his departure in January 1914: 'War can break out from one day to the next. . . . Our allies must rush to our aid. The safety of France will depend on the energy and promptness with which we shall know how to push them into the fight.'[17]

The visit of Poincaré was marred by extensive strikes in St. Petersburg and other large cities; Hans Rogger says of the industrial troubles in the capital in July 1914 that they 'raged for more than a week, required the use of troops to keep them out of the centre of the town, and revealed a degree of aggressiveness and exasperation on the part of the workers for which even sympathetic observers were unprepared.' Nevertheless some brilliant ceremonies and great military parades were calculated to impress the President with a sense of Russian power. On 21 July the wife of the Grand Duke Nicholas, a Montenegrin princess, declared gaily to Paléologue: 'There's going to be war. There'll be nothing left of Austria. . . . Our armies will meet in Berlin. Germany will be destroyed.'[18]

Although there was a war party at the Russian Court, there was also a peace party whose most influential advocate was Rasputin.

---

[16] E. M. Carroll, *French Public Opinion and Foreign Affairs, 1870–1914* (Harden, Conn., 1964), p. 291.

[17] M. Paléologue, *Journal 1913–14* (Paris, 1947), p. 269.

[18] Paléologue, *An Ambassador's Memoirs*, I, p. 23.

The *Staretz* had few political ideas, but he was quite certain that a great war would bring major disasters to the Russian Empire. However, in July 1914 Rasputin was off the board. He had gone on a visit to Siberia and on 29 June a prostitute stabbed him in the stomach and put him in hospital for several weeks. If Rasputin had been in St. Petersburg in the last week of July, it is possible that he would have exercised a restraining influence on the Tsar.

The French Government has never published any report on the important discussions between Poincaré and the Russian Government between 20 and 23 July, but it is clear that the President promised the full support of France in the impending international crisis. The British ambassador reported to Grey on 24 July that there was full agreement between France and Russia and that they had decided 'to take action at Vienna with a view to the prevention of a demand for explanations or any summons equivalent to an intervention in the internal affairs of Serbia which the latter would be justified in regarding as an attack on her sovereignty and independence'.[19] The Austrian ambassador, reporting a conversation with Poincaré on 21 July, referred to 'the threatening attitude of the President', sharply contrasting with that of Sazonov, and said this 'confirms the anticipation that M. Poincaré will exercise anything but a calming influence here'.

At 6 p.m. on 23 July, shortly after Poincaré and Viviani had sailed on their return voyage to France, the Austrian ultimatum was presented in Belgrade.

[19] This demolishes the contention of A. J. P. Taylor, *War by Time-Table* (London, 1969), p. 72 that Poincaré and Sazanov did not discuss Serbia during the President's visit. See also the revealing telegrams in Albertini II pp. 184–7 and pp. 190–5.

CHAPTER SIX

The Coming of War,
24 July–4 August 1914

SAZONOV heard of the Austrian ultimatum to Serbia at 10 a.m. on 24 July and at once exclaimed, '*C'est la guerre européenne!*' He immediately telephoned the news to the Tsar, who commented characteristically, 'this is disturbing.' After a tense discussion with the Austrian ambassador, Count Szapary, Sazonov sent for General Janushkevich, Chief of the General Staff, and discussed plans for a partial mobilization of the Russian Army. Standard histories of the crisis convey the impression that the conception of partial mobilization originated with the Foreign Minister, and Albertini describes it as, 'this bright idea of Sazonov's'. It is obvious, however, that Sazonov, who was pathetically ignorant of military affairs, was merely reviving the scheme for partial mobilization already formulated by Sukhomlinov in 1912 when Russia had come perilously close to plunging Europe into a major war.[1]

It is significant that Sazonov was contemplating something like a partial mobilization before the delivery of the Austrian ultimatum. On 18 July he told the British ambassador, Sir George Buchanan, that 'anything in the shape of an Austrian ultimatum at Belgrade could not leave Russia indifferent, and she might be forced to take some precautionary military measures.' It is highly probable that he discussed this question with the military leaders before 24 July, and that Sukhomlinov then submitted in extended form the proposal for partial mobilization which he had already formulated in 1912.

The proposal considered by Sazonov and Janushkevich on the 24th was to mobilize the Military Districts of Kiev, Odessa, Moscow and Kazan, but to refrain from mobilizing the Districts of Warsaw, Vilna and St. Petersburg in order to avoid alarming Germany. Sazonov certainly seems to have regarded this as an

[1] L. C. F. Turner, 'The Russian Mobilization in 1914', *JCH*, January 1968, pp. 70–1.

admirable way of exerting pressure on Austria; he did not understand that a partial mobilization involving thirteen Russian army corps along her northern border would compel Austria to order general mobilization, which in turn would invoke the Austro-German alliance and require general mobilization by Germany. Sazonov's ignorance was shared by Jagow, who told the British ambassador on 27 July that 'if Russia only mobilized in the south, Germany would not mobilize, but if she mobilized in the north, Germany would have to do so.' Jagow repeated the same statement to the French ambassador on the 27th and Albertini rightly describes his behaviour as 'a tremendous blunder', because 'partial mobilization would have led to war no less surely than general mobilization.'

Janushkevich was incapable of giving Sazonov sound advice. He had only been in office for five months and Sir Bernard Pares, who knew him personally, says 'he had nothing to recommend him but the personal favour of the Tsar.' Commenting on a letter written by Janushkevich in the summer of 1915, the Minister of Agriculture, Krivoshein, wrote: 'The extraordinary naïveté or, to be exact, the unforgiveable stupidity of this letter written by the Chief of Staff makes me shudder.' What neither Janushkevich nor Sukhomlinov ever understood was that it was very much to Russia's advantage to delay any mobilization until a substantial part of the Austrian Army was entangled in operations against Serbia. As we have seen, the possibility that Russia might do this was a source of great anxiety to Moltke and Conrad. Albertini rightly emphasizes that for Russia to bring diplomatic pressure to bear on Austria, it was unnecessary for her to mobilize; all that was required was that she should threaten to do so. He thus describes the Austrian dilemma:

> For Austria to take the field against Serbia it was needful, not only that Russia should not come in but that she should pledge herself *a priori* not to come in. Suppose that she had given no hint of any intention to mobilize and that Conrad after 1 August had sent towards the Save those four army corps that would have been needed in Galicia. Then if after 1 August Russia had gone over from words to deeds, Austria would not have had sufficient forces to meet her and the consequences might have been incalculable.[2]

Someone on the French General Staff understood this very well for the military memorandum submitted to Poincaré on 2

[2] Albertini, II, p. 482.

September 1912 had declared that a large-scale operation by Austria in the Balkans would have the effect of putting Germany and Austria 'at the mercy of the Entente'.[3] But Joffre, with his obsession about a Russian offensive towards Berlin, was not interested in the implications of the Austrian Plan B while General de Laguiche, the French military attaché in St. Petersburg, did nothing to enlighten the Russian General Staff on this matter. As a result Sazonov and the Russian generals failed to grasp the immense diplomatic and military advantages conferred on them by the Austrian dilemma.

The Russian Council of Ministers met at 3 p.m. on 24 July and came to the following decisions:

(1) A request to Austria for an extension of the ultimatum's time limit of forty-eight hours.

(2) Advice to Serbia not to engage in hostilities with Austria but to withdraw her troops. (On 24 July Sazonov sent a personal telegram, strongly tinged with panic, to his Belgrade legation and suggested that Serbia should surrender to Austria without fighting.)

(3) A request to the Tsar to authorize in principle the mobilization of the Military Districts of Kiev, Odessa, Moscow and Kazan and of the Baltic and Black Sea Fleets. (After the Council, the reference to the Baltic Fleet was inserted in the resolutions by the Tsar personally, although it ran directly counter to Sazonov's intention not to alarm Germany. Nothing illustrates more clearly the muddled character of Russian policy.)

(4) The Minister of War was urged to speed up the state of readiness of supplies and military equipment.

(5) Funds in Germany and Austria–Hungary were to be withdrawn.

The Austrian ultimatum shook the nerve of Pasich and the Serbian Government, and Albertini is probably correct in his contention that the Prime Minister's first impulse was to yield to the Austrian demands. Whether this would have deterred Austria from war is highly problematical but, by the afternoon of 25 July, a different spirit was prevailing in Belgrade. Encouraged by a report from his legation in St. Petersburg of the proceedings of the Russian Council of Ministers on 24 July and by an official Russian communiqué that Russia could not 'remain indifferent'

[3] See p. 36 above. This makes nonsense of the contention of the Fischer school that Germany was trying to provoke Russia 'by an Austrian *Blitzkrieg* in the Balkans'. Moltke was painfully aware that Russian intervention, while Austria was heavily engaged with Serbia, would be disastrous for the Central Powers.

to the fate of Serbia, Pasich resolved on a bolder policy. At 3 p.m. on 25 July Serbia ordered the mobilization of her Army, and that evening Baron Giesl, the Austrian minister in Belgrade, was handed a reply which an official in Vienna described as 'the most brilliant diplomatic document in my experience'. While very little in the ultimatum was rejected, very little was accepted and it would have required a lawyer of high repute to disentangle the real intentions of the Serbian Government. The article demanding the participation of Austrian officials in investigations on Serbian territory was rejected but the reply was so hedged around with reservations, apparent concessions and specious references to the Hague Tribunal that to Europe in general it gave an impression of abject acceptance. Even the Kaiser thought so when he first read the reply on the morning of 28 July.

Meanwhile Russia was proceeding to implement some very significant military measures, and there is no doubt that she was encouraged in this dangerous course by Maurice de Paléologue. On 24 July Sazonov and Buchanan lunched with the French ambassador. Sazonov expressed the opinion that 'Russia would at any rate have to mobilize' and Buchanan says in his report: 'The French ambassador gave me to understand that France would not only give Russia strong diplomatic support, but would, if necessary, fulfil the obligations imposed on her by the alliance.' According to Buchanan, Paléologue used strong language and gave the impression of being more decided than Sazonov.

A Russian Imperial Council, presided over by the Tsar and attended by the Grand Duke Nicholas and General Janushkevich, assembled at Krasnoe Selo on the morning of 25 July. The Grand Duke, who assumed command of the Russian Army on the outbreak of war, had given Joffre personal assurances that Russia would invade Germany as rapidly as possible; he was on bad terms with Sukhomlinov but got on well with Janushkevich, who served as his Chief of Staff in 1914–16 and was very much under his influence in the July crisis. The council approved the decisions taken on 24 July and adopted various resolutions. These included the return to winter quarters of troops on manoeuvres, the recall of officers on leave, and the promotion of cadets to be officers. Although the actual order for partial mobilization was still to be suspended, the Council decided to introduce immediately 'The Period Preparatory to War', over the whole of European

Russia. This corresponded with the German *Zustand drohender Kriegsgefahr* ('State of Threatening Danger of War'), and involved taking many measures preparatory to mobilization. Janushkevich sent out the relevant orders at 1 a.m. and 3.26 a.m. on 26 July, and thereby set in train a whole succession of military activities along the German and Austrian frontiers.

As a result, all fortresses in Poland and western Russia were placed in 'a state of war', frontier posts were fully manned, censorship and security measures were tightened, harbours were mined, horses and wagons were assembled for army baggage trains, depots were prepared for the reception of reservists and all steps were taken to facilitate the impending mobilization. These orders, already in force throughout European Russia, were extended on 27 July to include the Military Districts of the Caucasus, Turkestan, Omsk and Irkutsk.[4] Fay says: 'These secret "preparatory measures" ... ordered before dawn of the 26th, enabled Russia, when war came, to surprise the world by the rapidity with which she poured her troops into East Prussia and Galicia.' In the light of Russian actions between 24 and 26 July it seems extraordinary that an historian of Fischer's repute should seriously maintain that Bethmann Hollweg's calculations were upset in July 1914 by Russia's 'unexpected backing down'.[5]

These far-reaching military decisions may well have been influenced by the critical internal situation, and the wave of strikes then threatening to paralyse Russian industry and transport. The German ambassador, Count Pourtalès, reported on 25 July: 'From a trustworthy source I hear that in the Ministerial Council here yesterday [24 July] the question of first consideration discussed was whether the present internal situation of Russia is such that the country could face external complications without trouble.'

On the evening of the 25th, in conversation with the Italian ambassador, Paléologue declared that war was virtually inevitable and expressed his approval of the decisions taken that day at the Imperial Council. He added that, 'France was ready to fulfil her duty as an ally to the full.' Albertini admits that France was bound to give Russia diplomatic support, but comments very reasonably:

---

[4] A. von Wegerer, *Der Ausbruch des Weltkrieges 1914* (Hamburg, 1943), II, p. 15, quoting Russian documents.
[5] Fischer, *Weltmacht oder Niedergang*, pp. 58–9.

But she was in a position to have exercised friendly restraint and proffered councils of prudence which might have averted the catastrophe. What the French representative at St. Petersburg did was, on the contrary, to fan the flames, and thus expose his own country to the most serious risk . . . [6]

On 25 July Paléologue informed Paris that the Tsar had approved in principle the mobilization of thirteen army corps against Austria, and on the 26th his military attaché, General de Laguiche, reported as follows to the French Ministry of War:

Yesterday at Krasnoe Selo the War Minister confirmed to me the mobilization of the army corps of the military districts Kiev, Odessa, Kazan and Moscow. The endeavour is to avoid any measure likely to be regarded as directed against Germany, but nevertheless the military districts of Warsaw, Vilna and St. Petersburg are secretly making preparations. The cities and governments of St. Petersburg and Moscow are declared to be under martial law. . . . The Minister of War has reiterated to us his determination to leave to Germany the eventual initiative of an attack on Russia . . . [7]

Although the order for partial mobilization had yet to be promulgated, this singular document indicates that Sukhomlinov regarded the mobilization proclamation as a mere formality which would follow automatically after the preliminary measures covered in 'The Period Preparatory to War' had been completed. This adds significance to the statement by General Dobrorolski, Chief of the Mobilization Section of the Russian General Staff, who says of the situation in Russia on 26 July: 'The war was already a settled matter, and the whole flood of telegrams between the Governments of Russia and Germany represented merely the stage setting of a historical drama.'[8] He admits that local commanders may well have gone beyond the letter of the regulations and introduced measures of mobilization, and he mentions such cases in the Suwalki area bordering East Prussia.

While the Russian military machine was gathering pace along the road to war, some fateful decisions were being taken in Vienna and Berlin. Baron Giesl had not troubled to read the Serbian reply, but broke off relations and left immediately for

---

[6] Albertini, II, pp. 626–7.

[7] *DDF* 3 XI, No. 89. This significant document is omitted by Geiss from his *Julikrise und Kriegsausbruch 1914*, 2 vols. (Hannover, 1963–4).

[8] S. Dobrorolski, *Die Mobilmachung der russischen Armee, 1914* (Berlin, 1922), pp. 21–2.

Vienna. On the evening of 25 July Austria ordered the mobilization of seven army corps against Serbia while another corps (based on Graz) was mobilized as a precaution against Italy, whom Conrad profoundly distrusted. This did not mean that Conrad was irrevocably committed to Plan B – he still had until 1 August to decide whether Plan B or Plan R would be implemented. After 1 August it would be too late to change, and Conrad would have no alternative but to allow the troop trains carrying the four corps of his Second Army to roll on to the Danube frontier. If the Second Army was wanted in Galicia, it would have to be brought back all the way from the Serbian border.

The actions of the Berlin 'statesmen' were singularly maladroit. Jagow and Zimmermann deceived no one with their childish pretence that Germany had no previous knowledge of the ultimatum, while Bethmann Hollweg directed his ambassadors in St. Petersburg, London and Paris to inform the respective governments that, 'We urgently desire the localization of the conflict because any intervention by another Power would in consequence of the various alliance obligations bring incalculable consequences in its train.' The French Press reacted sharply to this implied 'threat of war', and stated quite correctly that the balance of power in Europe was at stake and France must support Russia.

The reaction of the British Foreign Office is reflected in Sir Eyre Crowe's comments to Grey on Sir George Buchanan's telegram of 24 July: 'The moment has passed when it might have been possible to enlist French support in an effort to hold back Russia. ... It is clear that France and Russia are decided to accept the challenge thrown out to them.' After talking to Grey on the evening of the 24th, Prince Lichnowsky reported that the Foreign Secretary 'was greatly affected by the Austrian note which, according to his view, exceeded anything he had ever seen of this sort before'. Grey expressed grave fears of Russian intervention and the prospect of a general European war. The Italian reaction is shown by the note addressed by San Giuliano, the Foreign Minister, to his ambassadors in Berlin and Vienna, 'By the style in which the [Austrian] note is couched and the demands it contains ... Austria has plainly shown that she means to provoke a war. ... Italy is under no obligation to go to the help of Austria in case that, as a result of this *démarche* of hers, she finds herself at war with Russia ....'

The situation on 25/26 July was already very dangerous, but perhaps it was not too late for Germany to draw back from the precipice. If Bethmann Hollweg had possessed an atom of political judgment, he would have waited to test the reactions of Europe to the Austrian ultimatum and the partial mobilization against Serbia. Instead he plunged into the desperate course of confronting Europe with the *fait accompli* of an Austrian declaration of war on Serbia and the opening of hostilities against her. He and Jagow were adhering blindly to the doctrine proclaimed by the Foreign Minister in his letter to Lichnowsky of 18 July, 'the more boldness Austria displays, the more strongly we support her, the more likely is Russia to keep quiet.'

On the morning of 26 July Berchtold summoned Conrad and Tschirschky to his office and informed them of a telegram he had received from Count Szögyeny, the Austrian ambassador in Berlin. Tschirschky's report of the discussion, despatched to Berlin at 4.50 p.m. on the 26th, reads as follows:

> Count Berchtold read out to me Count Szögyeny's telegram saying that to avoid the risk as far as possible of intervention by third parties Berlin regarded the greatest speed in military operations and the earliest declaration of war as advisable. The Minister had already summoned Baron von Hötzendorf to discuss this point and he appeared while I was with the Minister. To the Chief of Staff I warmly advocated our standpoint which was fully shared by Count Berchtold. Baron von Hötzendorf explained that it was vital to avoid opening the campaign with inadequate forces. . . . He reckoned on beginning the general advance about 12 August. However, a formal declaration of war would probably prove superfluous since he assumed that in the next few days armed Serbian incursions across the Bosnian frontier would occur.

According to Conrad's account, after the German ambassador's departure, the conversation ran as follows:

> Berchtold: 'We should like to send the declaration of war to Serbia as soon as possible in order that various influences may cease. When do you want the declaration of war?'
> Conrad: 'Only when we are at the stage when operations can begin at once – say on 12 August.'
> Berchtold: 'The diplomatic situation will not hold so long. One cannot be sure that there will not be clashes at the frontier.'[9]

[9] Conrad, *Aus meiner Dienstzeit*, IV, pp. 131–2, and *DD* No. 213. The translation of *DD* No. 213 in Albertini, II, p. 454, is gravely misleading, cf. Geiss *July 1914*, pp. 228–9.

After further discussion, they decided to postpone the declaration of war on Serbia. Conrad stressed that the declaration was not urgent; no serious operations could be launched against Serbia until the mobilization of his invading forces was complete, and this could not happen until 12 August. It was only after persistent pressure by Berchtold on 27 July and references to the effect desired by Germany of 'confronting the world with a *fait accompli*', that Conrad gave his consent to a declaration of war 'provided diplomatic considerations made it seem necessary'. Summing up this phase of the crisis, Albertini says that 'Austria declared war on Serbia against the advice of the Austrian Chief of Staff and under German pressure.'[10]

Meanwhile Bethmann was being subjected to pressure from Sir Edward Grey to accept mediation. Unfortunately Grey endeavoured to make a distinction between an Austro-Serbian conflict, which he declared was not a direct concern of Britain, and an Austro-Russian one. Like every other Foreign Secretary in Europe, he showed a complete misunderstanding of the significance of mobilization; indeed in conversation with the Russian ambassador on 25 July he assumed as a matter of course that Russia would mobilize against Austria. A blunt statement to Germany on 26 July that Britain would be sure to intervene on the side of France might have deterred Bethmann Hollweg from pushing Austria into her suicidal declaration of war on Serbia, but no specific warning was forthcoming from Grey until 29 July. Grey's apologists have maintained that he could take no positive step without Cabinet approval, but this is belied by the fact that he did not seek Cabinet approval for his *démarche* of 29 July. In any case, it would not have been easy for Grey to warn Germany on 26 July, because he departed for his usual weekend in the country on the afternoon of the 25th.

On 24/25 July Grey did attempt to induce Germany to accept the principle of mediation of Britain, Germany, France and Italy between Austria and Russia. Lichnowsky urged Berlin to accept, as 'the only possibility of avoiding a world war in which we should risk everything and gain nothing' and added that he did not believe in the possibility of British neutrality. Albertini is quite correct in saying that the apparent acceptance of this offer by Bethmann and Jagow was a manoeuvre designed to deceive the British. The breaking-off of relations between Austria

[10] Albertini, II, p. 457 *n*. See also Taylor, *War by Time-Table*, p. 80.

and Serbia created a new situation, and Sir Arthur Nicolson persuaded Grey to ask Germany to agree to a conference of ambassadors in London, similar to the one which had handled the Balkan disputes of 1912–13, except that Austria and Russia would be excluded. The proposal was telegraphed to Berlin on the evening of 26 July and rejected by Bethmann Hollweg in a telegram to Lichnowsky at 1 p.m. on the 27th which read: 'We could not take part in such a conference as we cannot drag Austria in her conflict with Serbia before a European tribunal.'

In conversation with Lichnowsky on the morning of 27 July, Grey proposed that Berlin should induce Vienna to accept the Serbian reply as a basis for negotiations in order to prevent a war which 'would be the biggest ever known'. Lichnowsky's urgent appeal that the request should be accepted made some impression in Berlin, especially as it was coupled with news that the British Fleet, assembled for a test mobilization at Portland, was under orders not to disperse. Grey's proposal was passed on to Vienna at 11.50 p.m. on 27 July, but the Austrian ambassador in Berlin informed Berchtold: 'The German Government assures us in the most decided way that it does not identify itself with these propositions; that on the contrary it advises that they be disregarded, but that it must pass them on to satisfy the English Government.' Albertini concludes that 'all the Chancellor sought to do was to throw dust in the eyes of Grey and lead him to believe that Berlin was seriously trying to avoid a conflict, that if war broke out it would be Russia's fault and that England could therefore remain neutral.'[11]

The gravest indictment against German policy in July 1914 rests on the conduct of Bethmann Hollweg on the 27th. By this time it was becoming apparent that any prospect of localizing an Austro-Serbian conflict was illusory. The recall of all officers from leave in France, the holding together of the British Fleet, and the alarming reports of military activity in Russia indicated that the Triple Entente was preparing for war. It is absurd for the Fischer school to contend that Bethmann thought that Russia was 'backing down', in view of the detailed reports pouring into Berlin about her military preparations. As early as 26 July Sir Edward Grey noted: 'Prince Lichnowsky called this afternoon with an urgent telegram from his Government to say that they had received information that Russia was calling in "classes of

[11] Ibid., II, pp. 444–5.

reserves", which meant mobilization'. At 3.25 p.m. on 26 July, Pourtalès telegraphed to Jagow that Major Eggeling, the German military attaché in St. Petersburg, had reported that mobilization had certainly been ordered for the Military Districts of Kiev and Odessa, but it was doubtful whether this had been done for Warsaw and Moscow. On the evening of the 26th Pourtalès interviewed Sazonov and was assured that 'no mobilization order of the sort had been issued' but that certain military measures had been taken.

On the evening of 26 July Sukhomlinov sent for Major Eggeling and gave him his 'word of honour that no mobilization order had yet been issued'. He asserted that only preparatory measures were being taken, but that 'not a horse was being requisitioned, not a reservist called up'. If Austria invaded Serbia the Districts of Kiev, Odessa, Moscow and Kazan would be mobilized, but in no circumstances would this be done at Warsaw, Vilna or St. Petersburg as 'peace with Germany was urgently desired'. Eggeling's report continues:

> Upon my inquiry as to the object of the mobilization against Austria, he shrugged his shoulders and indicated the diplomats ... I got the impression of great nervousness and anxiety. I consider the wish for peace genuine, military statements so far correct, that complete mobilization has probably not been ordered, but preparatory measures are very far-reaching. They are evidently striving to gain time for new negotiations and for continuing their armaments. Also the internal situation is unmistakably causing serious anxiety.

Eggeling warned Sukhomlinov that even 'mobilization against Austria alone must be regarded as very dangerous.'

This report was received in Berlin at 2.35 a.m. on 27 July and should have left the Chancellor under no illusions about the probable reaction in St. Petersburg to an Austrian declaration of war on Serbia. There is, however, strong reason to believe that Bethmann was now resigning himself to the inevitability of war with France and Russia and was gambling on British neutrality. The great object of his policy was to saddle Russia with the responsibility for aggression – firstly to affect British opinion and secondly to rally the Social Democrats in Germany in support of a war for the defence of the German Fatherland.[12]

[12] E. Zechlin, 'Bethmann Hollweg, Kriegsrisiko und SPD 1914'. *Der Monat*, 19, 1966, p. 23 *et seq*. At the meeting of the Prussian Cabinet on 30 July 1914, Bethmann was able to assure members: 'Even from Social Democracy and the

Bethmann's treatment of the Kaiser is one of the most singular aspects of the crisis. Telegrams to the *Hohenzollern* deliberately played down the gravity of the situation and news was transmitted in a garbled, uninformative style. In spite of the Kaiser's blustering marginal notes and furious denunciations of Serbia, Bethmann and Jagow feared with good reason that Wilhelm's nerve might crack at any moment and did all they could to keep him away from Berlin. In this they were unsuccessful. Contrary to the Chancellor's express advice, the Kaiser ordered the High Seas Fleet to abandon its Norwegian cruise and return to Kiel on 26 July, while he himself headed for Potsdam in a state of great nervous agitation.

Moltke had returned to his office in Berlin on the morning of 26 July, and his first act was to draft the text of the ultimatum to Belgium to be presented in Brussels in the event of war. This does not mean that the Chief of Staff thought that hostilities were imminent. Writing to his wife on the morning of 27 July he said, '. . . the situation continues to be extremely obscure. . . . It will be about another fortnight before anything definite can be known or said.' Moltke knew that Austria could not begin operations against Serbia before 12 August, and his letter shows that Bethmann Hollweg had not told him about the pressure he was exerting in Vienna for an early declaration of war on Serbia.

Fuming with indignation against his Chancellor for keeping him in the dark and questioning his orders to the Fleet, the Kaiser returned to Potsdam at 3 p.m. on 27 July. That afternoon he conferred with Bethmann, Jagow and Moltke, and the diary of Admiral von Müller, Chief of his Naval Cabinet, records: 'The tenor of our policy is to remain calm. To allow Russia to put herself in the wrong, but then not to shrink from war if it were inevitable.'[13] Not only did Bethmann and Jagow conceal the text of the Serbian reply to the Austrian ultimatum from the Kaiser, but they remained silent about Austria's impending declaration of war. Tschirschky's telegram reporting this arrived in Berlin at 4.37 p.m. on 27 July: 'It has been decided here to send official

---

SPD leadership nothing of any consequence was to be feared; this he felt entitled to say after negotiations with the Reichstag deputy, Südekum. Of a general or partial strike or sabotage there would be no question'. (*DD* No. 456).

[13] W. Goerlitz (ed.), *The Kaiser and his Court* (London, 1961), p. 7.

declaration of war tomorrow, at latest the day after, in order to cut away the ground from any attempt at intervention.' This news was not sent on to Potsdam; the text of the Serbian reply was despatched at 9.30 p.m. but by the time it arrived at the Neues Palais the Kaiser had gone to bed. When he read the reply on the morning of the 28th Wilhelm penned his famous comment:

A brilliant achievement in a time limit of only forty-eight hours! It is more than one could have expected! A great moral success for Vienna; but with it all reason for war disappears and Giesl ought to have quietly stayed on in Belgrade! After that I should never have ordered mobilization.

The Kaiser declared that he was willing to mediate on the basis of a temporary Austrian occupation of Belgrade. But at 11 a.m. within an hour of the Kaiser's change of front, Berchtold was telegraphing the Austrian declaration of war on Serbia to Nish, where the Serbian Government was now located.

The Austrian declaration of war was received with tremendous enthusiasm in Vienna, warmly applauded in Berlin, and violently denounced in Russia in a paroxysm of popular fury. Although Paris remained superficially calm, excitement was rising and it is reasonable to assume that the actions and judgment of statesmen and soldiers were profoundly modified by the tremendous surge of public opinion and the flaming headlines and comments of the daily Press.

With the Austrian declaration of war, the crisis entered its final phase and the potential application of the Schlieffen Plan dominated the situation. Nowhere was this more apparent than in Paris. The diplomatic activity of the French Government between 23 and 29 July was virtually paralysed by the absence of Poincaré and Viviani, who was both Prime Minister and Foreign Minister, on their return voyage from the Gulf of Finland, but the Ministry of War was already taking extensive precautions. On 26 July all officers were recalled from leave and steps were taken to protect the railways, while on the 27th nearly 100,000 troops were summoned from Morocco and Algeria. The telegrams from Paléologue and Laguiche on 25/26 July, reporting the contemplated Russian partial mobilization against Austria, raised the whole question of the military conventions between France and Russia and stirred Joffre into vigorous action. The Chief of Staff describes the steps he took on 27 July:

The direction which events were taking left me with no illusion – we were headed straight for war and Russia was going to find herself drawn in at the same time as ourselves. My first thought, therefore, was to strengthen the liaison between us and our Allies and I asked the Minister [of War] to endeavour through all possible means to make sure that, if hostilities broke out, the Government of St. Petersburg, would immediately take the offensive in East Prussia, as had been agreed upon in our conventions.[14]

Messimy, the Minister of War, relates that as a result of this request he communicated with General de Laguiche at St. Petersburg on 27 July and 'urged with all my might that, in spite of the slowness of Russian mobilization, the Tsar's armies should as soon as possible take the offensive in East Prussia'.[15] On 28 July Joffre and Messimy saw Colonel Ignatiev, the Russian military attaché in Paris, and impressed on him that France was fully prepared to fulfil her alliance obligations.

The pressure which Joffre and Messimy were exerting in St. Petersburg was calculated to drive the Russian General Staff into demanding general mobilization. Moreover, Paléologue continued to exert all in his influence in favour of extreme measures. On 27 July Viviani had telegraphed to him from the warship *France*, stressing the need to make every effort to secure a peaceful solution. So far from advocating this course to Sazonov, Paléologue assured him on the 28th of the 'complete readiness of France to fulfil her obligations as an ally in case of necessity'.

Although historians have frequently asserted that the Russian General Staff was driven into demanding general mobilization, because of the technical impossibility of carrying out partial mobilization, yet this belief has no validity.[16] From a military point of view it would have been quite possible for Russia to carry out a partial mobilization, but this would still have led to a major war because Austria would have been compelled by the threat to her defenceless northern frontier to respond with general mobilization, thus invoking the Austro-German alliance.

The news of the Austrian declaration of war on Serbia infuriated Sazonov. Encouraged by Paléologue and moved by

---

[14] J. J. C. Joffre, *Memoirs of Marshal Joffre* (London, 1932), I, pp. 117–8.

[15] R. Recouly, *Les Heures tragiques d'avant guerre* (Paris, 1922), pp. 69–70.

[16] L. C. F. Turner, 'The Russian Mobilization in 1914', *JCH*, January 1968, pp. 72–4. Partial mobilization would have imposed some delay on a general mobilization.

what Baron Taube describes as 'the pathological nervosity of his nature', he despatched the following telegram on the evening of 28 July to Berlin, repeated to Vienna, Paris, London and Rome:

> In consequence of the Austrian declaration of war on Serbia, we shall tomorrow proclaim mobilization in the districts of Odessa, Kiev, Moscow and Kazan. Inform the German Government of this and lay stress on the absence of any intention on the part of Russia to attack Germany.

Presumably this telegram was sent with the permission of the Tsar. However, that night Janushkevich sent a very different telegram to the commanders of all Military Districts: '30 July will be proclaimed the first day of our general mobilization. The proclamation will follow by the regulation telegram.'[17] In a telegram to the Kaiser at 1 a.m. on 29 July, the Tsar appealed for his help to try and avoid a European war and remarked: 'I foresee that very soon I shall be overwhelmed by the pressure brought upon me and be forced to take extreme measures which will lead to war.' Matters were rapidly getting out of control, and the events of 29 July were to compromise hopelessly the slender prospects of maintaining peace.

On 29 July Moltke presented a memorandum to the Chancellor and warned him that Russian military measures directed against Austria would lead to Austrian general mobilization. Moltke said: 'The instant Austria mobilizes her whole Army, the clash between her and Russia will become inevitable. Now that is for Germany the *casus foederis* . . . she must also mobilize.' However, Moltke's language was far from being that of an ardent militarist thirsting for war. On the contrary, he predicted that Austrian and German general mobilization would bring the Franco-Russian alliance into operation and then 'the civilized states of Europe would begin to tear one another to pieces.' Moltke said: 'This is the way things will and must develop, unless, one might almost say, a miracle takes place to prevent at the eleventh hour a war which will annihilate the civilization of almost the whole of Europe for decades to come.'

As a result of Moltke's memorandum, Bethmann Hollweg telegraphed to Count Pourtalès at 12.50 p.m. on 29 July: 'Kindly impress on M. Sazonov very seriously that further continuation of Russian mobilization measures would compel us to mobilize

[17] Albertini, II, p. 545. This is one of the key documents not published by Geiss.

and that then European war could scarcely be prevented.' Stressing that this was 'not a threat but a friendly opinion', Pourtalès passed the message on to Sazonov at about 7 p.m., with consequences which can only be described as catastrophic. The Foreign Minister had spent the day engaged in an unending series of conversations with ambassadors and, in his muddled way, still seems to have had some hopes of preserving peace. While he was doing this, General Dobrorolski was getting the signature of the War Minister, Navy Minister and Minister of the Interior to the *ukaze* for general mobilization, while at Russian Army Headquarters the necessary telegrams were being prepared, ready for despatch to the farthest parts of the Empire. News of the bombardment of Belgrade by Austrian monitors came in that afternoon and, for the excitable and unstable Sazonov, Pourtalès' communication was the last straw. He immediately sought the Tsar's permission to call a conference with Sukhomlinov and Janushkevich to decide on mobilization, and the official diary of the Russian Foreign Ministry records:

> After examining the situation from all points, both the Ministers [Sazonov and Sukhomlinov] and the Chief of the General Staff decided that in view of the small probability of avoiding a war with Germany it was indispensable to prepare for it in every way in good time, and that therefore the risk could not be accepted of delaying a general mobilization later by effecting a partial mobilization now. The conclusion reached at this conference was at once reported by telephone to the Tsar, who authorized the taking of steps accordingly. This information was received with enthusiasm by the small circle of those acquainted with what was in progress.

Between 9.30 and 10 p.m. on 29 July, General Dobrorolski was at the central telegraph office in St. Petersburg ready to despatch the general mobilization order. He was just about to do so, when Janushkevich telephoned him to suspend it pending the arrival of a liaison officer. The latter reported that the Tsar had cancelled general mobilization and substituted partial mobilization instead. The Tsar's change of mind resulted from a telegram from the Kaiser received at 9.40 p.m., appealing for the Tsar's co-operation in averting a catastrophe. Saying, 'I will not be responsible for a monstrous slaughter', Nicholas insisted on the cancellation. The partial mobilization order was telegraphed to the relevant Military Districts at midnight.

While these dramatic events were proceeding in St. Petersburg

Bethmann Hollweg was receiving shattering news from London. Hopes of British neutrality had risen as a result of an optimistic report by Prince Henry of Prussia of a conversation with George V on 26 July and on the evening of the 29th Bethmann committed the supreme stupidity of telling the British ambassador that, if Britain remained neutral, Germany would take no territory from France although she could give no such guarantee for the French colonies. That very afternoon, however, Grey warned Lichnowsky of the probability of British intervention, and stated quite frankly that if France was involved in war with Germany 'the British Government would under the circumstances find itself forced to take rapid decisions. In that event it would not be practicable to stand aside and wait for any length of time.'

Whatever may be thought of Albertini's view that Grey should have spoken in this fashion at an earlier stage, it is certain that Lichnowsky's report of 29 July had a tremendous impact in Berlin. The warning was reinforced by reports of Britain's naval mobilization, which were already causing panic on the Berlin Stock Exchange.[18] According to Tirpitz, Bethmann was now showing signs of 'complete collapse', and Lichnowksy's telegram, received at 9.12 p.m., sounded the death knell of the policy of 'localization'. On the night of 29/30 July the Chancellor made desperate efforts to reverse the whole trend of German policy since 5 July, and sent telegrams to Vienna urging restraint and negotiations with Russia. There is no justification for questioning the sincerity of Bethmann's messages, which Albertini likens to a drowning man clutching at a lifebuoy. In a telegram despatched to Tschirschky at 3 a.m. on 30 July, Bethmann said:

. . . the refusal of all exchange of views with St. Petersburg would be a grave error, since it would provoke armed intervention by Russia which it is, more than anything, to Austria–Hungary's interest to avoid.

We are of course ready to fulfil our duty as allies, but must decline to let ourselves be dragged by Vienna, wantonly and without regard to our advice, into a world conflagration.

Albertini comments: 'Things had come to such a pass that it would have needed a very different approach to make the men

[18] On the night 29/30 July the British First Fleet proceeded through the Straits of Dover to its war station at Scapa Flow.

at Vienna understand that they must go no further on the road along which they had advanced with the consent and at the insistence of Germany.'[19]

The last hopes of peace vanished on 30 July. At St. Petersburg, Laguiche and Paléologue were gravely disturbed at the failure to order general mobilization and redoubled their clamour for warlike measures against Germany. A telegram despatched by Viviani from Paris at 7 a.m. on 30 July impressed on Paléologue that Russia should not immediately take any step which might offer Germany a pretext for a total or partial mobilization of her forces. It arrived too late to influence events and, in any case, was effectively throttled by the ambassador. During the day Sazonov, Sukhomlinov and Janushkevich exerted all the pressure in their power on the Tsar and on the afternoon of the 30th Sazonov won his reluctant consent to the proclamation of general mobilization. The significance of the Tsar's change of mind has been much exaggerated; the fatal Russian decision had been taken on 29 July, for partial mobilization would have led to war as surely as general mobilization.

The news of Russian partial mobilization was received in Berlin on the morning of 30 July, and during the next few hours Moltke's mood underwent a decisive change. Hitherto the attitude of the German Chief of Staff had been restrained; he had done nothing to hamper Bethmann Hollweg's belated attempt to put the brake on Austria and, at conferences on 29 July, he had not pressed for German mobilization.[20] Even on the morning of the 30th he told Captain Fleischmann, the Austrian liaison officer with the German General Staff, that Russian partial mobilization was no reason for German mobilization. Yet by 1 p.m. on the 30th Moltke was pressing Bethmann Hollweg for the immediate proclamation of *drohende Kriegsgefahr*, the first stage of general mobilization. He was unable to persuade the distracted Chancellor and returned from the interview in a state of 'great agitation'.

There has been much speculation about the reasons for Moltke's change of mind. No doubt the increasing gravity of the general situation affected him considerably, but the decisive

[19] Albertini, II, p. 526, commenting on *DD* No. 396. Bethmann was also upset by the increasing certainty of Italian neutrality. See particularly *DD* No. 340.

[20] Ibid., II, pp. 490–2, and III, p. 7.

factor appears to have been news from Vienna that Conrad intended to adhere rigidly to Plan B, and did not propose to abandon that plan in the light of Russian partial mobilization. In a telegram to Berlin drafted at 7.30 p.m. on 30 July Conrad declared that Austrian general mobilization was imminent but the Austrian armies in Galicia would have a defensive role while the attack on Serbia would proceed; in a telephone message to Berlin on the afternoon of the 31st he confirmed that he intended to stand on the defensive against Russia and proceed with the punitive action against Serbia.[21] These messages were preceded by a minute from the Austrian ambassador to Jagow on the afternoon of 30 July, and the implications for Germany were catastrophic. Unless Austria fully committed herself to Plan R and launched a great offensive in Poland, the German Eighth Army in East Prussia would be overwhelmed by the Russian masses and the prospects for the success of the Schlieffen Plan would be hopelessly compromised. This explains the excited conversations between Moltke and Lieut-Colonel Bienerth, the Austrian military attaché, on the afternoon of 30 July and the frantic telegrams sent by them to Vienna that evening, urging immediate mobilization against Russia and promising unqualified German support in a European war which was declared to be 'the last means of preserving Austria–Hungary'.

The tone of these telegrams ran directly counter to the efforts which Bethmann Hollweg was then making to restrain Austria and persuade her to negotiate. On 31 July these contradictory exhortations drew the sarcastic comment from Berchtold, 'who rules in Berlin, Moltke or Bethmann?' Berchtold said to members of the Imperial War Council that morning: 'I have sent for you because I had the impression that Germany was beating a retreat, but I now have the most reassuring pronouncement from responsible military quarters.' The Council then decided to submit the order for general mobilization to the Emperor Franz Josef for signature.

Russian and Austrian general mobilization made a great war inevitable and Liddell Hart says: 'Henceforth the "statesmen" may continue to send telegrams, but they are merely waste

---

[21] Ibid., II, p. 672, DD No. 427 and Ritter, 'Der Anteil der Militärs an der Kriegskatastrophe von 1914'. *HZ* 1961, 193, pp. 86–7. Conrad did not cancel Plan B until 5 August, with the result that his Second Army was transported to the Serbian frontier and arrived too late at the disastrous Battle of Lemberg.

paper. The military machine has completely taken charge.'[22] As soon as Moltke learned of Russian general mobilization on the morning of 31 July, he not only insisted on the immediate proclamation of *Kriegsgefahr* in Berlin, but induced the Chancellor to despatch an ultimatum to St. Petersburg demanding that Russia should cease all military measures against Germany and Austria–Hungary within twelve hours. In the absence of a reply, Germany declared war on Russia at 6 p.m. on 1 August. Gerhard Ritter explains this 'unbelievable haste' by the need to capture Liège at the very outset of the war, and comments:

> In other words: the gamble of the Schlieffen Plan was so great that it could only succeed as a result of a rapid surprise advance by the Germans or by a sudden onslaught on Belgium. In the opinion of the General Staff, Germany was therefore obliged by purely technical necessities to adopt before the whole world, the role of a brutal aggressor – an evil moral burden which, as is well known, we have not got rid of even today.[23]

On the evening of 2 August an ultimatum requesting passage for the German armies was delivered in Brussels; King Albert and his Government categorically rejected the demand on the morning of the 3rd. Meanwhile on the evening of the 1st Baron von Schoen, the German ambassador in Paris, had asked Viviani how France intended to act in a Russo-German war and received the reply that 'France would act as her interests required'. Both France and Germany proclaimed general mobilization on the evening of the 1st, and Germany declared war on France at 6.45 p.m. on 3 August; the declaration was justified by lying statements about French frontier violations and a bombing attack on Nuremberg.

The British Cabinet had been deeply divided since 27 July when Grey 'in his quiet way' informed his colleagues that the time had come to decide between intervention and neutrality, and said 'if the choice was for neutrality, he was not the man to carry it out.'[24] Whatever he may have written in his memoirs, Lloyd George's attitude towards British obligations to Belgium remained pretty ambiguous until 3 August, while there was a strong non-intervention group in the Cabinet of whom Lord

[22] B. H. Liddell Hart, *A History of the World War 1914–1918* (London, 1934), p. 47.

[23] Ritter, article *HZ*, 1961, 193, pp. 89–90.

[24] Lord Morley's account quoted by Gooch p. 376.

Morley and John Burns were the most prominent spokesmen. Grey himself made a very serious slip on 1 August, when he indicated to Lichnowsky that, if Germany refrained from attacking France, Britain would remain neutral and guarantee French passivity.[25] In Berlin the report made such an impression that the Kaiser even ordered Moltke to suspend the German advance into Luxemburg and exclaimed, 'we march then with all our forces towards the east.' Albertini surmises that under the strain of events, Grey 'lost his head' – perhaps he was affected by the collapse of the Stock Exchange and predictions of dire financial catastrophe in the City. Although the incident was soon clarified and is not of major importance, it does illustrate the lack of coherence in British policy and the acute tensions in the Cabinet.

By 2 August the French ambassador, Paul Cambon, was asking 'whether the word "honour" should not be struck out of the English vocabulary'. However, on the 2nd Britain gave France an assurance that the High Seas Fleet would not be permitted to enter the Channel and attack the unprotected ports of northern France. That evening the Cabinet decided that any violation of Belgian neutrality would oblige Britain to intervene. According to Asquith's biographer, J. A. Spender, the decision was not taken without 'heavy wrestling', and some ministers endeavoured to argue that a 'simple traverse' of a corner of Belgium would not justify Britain in going to war.[26] In the event only Morley and Burns resigned from the Cabinet, while the Conservative Party pledged Asquith their full support.

German troops crossed the Belgian frontier on the morning of 4 August; a British ultimatum requesting their withdrawal was disregarded and at 11 p.m. on the 4th Britain and Germany were at war.

[25] Albertini, III, pp. 380–5. The incident precipitated *DD*. No. 562.

[26] J. A. Spender, *Life of Herbert Henry Asquith, Lord Oxford and Asquith* (London, 1932), II, pp. 89–91. See also the discussion in R. Jenkins, *Asquith* (London, 1964), pp. 325–9. Jenkins believes that, even on the morning of 1 August, half the Cabinet was ready to oppose the sending of an ultimatum to Germany.

Conclusion

EARLY in August 1914 Prince von Bülow called on Bethmann Hollweg in the Chancellor's Palace in Berlin. He thus describes his reception:

> Bethmann stood in the centre of the room. Shall I ever forget his face. . . . There is a picture by some celebrated English painter, which shows the wretched scapegoat with a look of ineffable anguish in its eyes – such pain as I now saw in Bethmann's. For an instant we neither of us spoke. At last I said to him: 'Well, tell me, at least, how it all happened.' He raised his long, thin arms to heaven and answered in a dull, exhausted voice: 'Oh – if I only knew!' In many later polemics on 'war guilt' I have often wished it had been possible to produce a snapshot of Bethmann Hollweg . . . at the moment he said those words. Such a photograph would have been the best proof that this wretched man had never 'wanted war'.[1]

Whatever war aims they proclaimed during the conflict, none of the rulers of the Great Powers really knew what they were fighting about in August 1914. Once the Austrian ultimatum had been delivered in Belgrade, the crisis gathered momentum and the calculations of statesmen were overwhelmed by the rapid succession of events, the tide of emotion in the various capitals, and the inexorable demands of military planning. After the first great battles, the leading political figures soon lost contact with reality, while popular demands for victory and vengeance insisted on a ruthless prosecution of the war and the imposition of a merciless peace on the conquered enemy. Germany perhaps surpassed other powers in pursuing extravagant war aims, and no doubt the origins of some of the plans formulated in the Reich in 1914–18 can be traced to the pre-war years. This applies particularly to the famous 'September Programme', approved by Bethmann Hollweg before the Battle of the Marne was decided and embodying features of the *Mitteleuropa* conception submitted to the Chancellor by Walther Rathenau in August 1914.[2] Moses argues that this demonstrates 'the naked German will to power';

---

[1] Bülow, *Memoirs 1909–1919*, p. 145. The reference is to Holman Hunt's masterpiece 'The Scapegoat'.

[2] Fischer, *Germany's Aims in the First World War*, p. 11 and pp. 100–3.

certainly the Chancellor and his entourage were intoxicated by the great victories of the Frontiers and Tannenberg, but there is little evidence for the assumption that Germany deliberately went to war in order to realize the policies set out in the September Programme and similar documents.

Fischer has rendered a great service to historical knowledge by his thoroughly documented study of German war aims, but P. H. S. Hatton has pointed out that 'once embarked upon a war, states in both alliance-groups thought in terms of what they might gain if the war was won.' He draws attention to the 'surprising speed' with which the British Colonial Office decided in August 1914 that 'Germany's colonies in Africa must be forfeit, if possible to Britain.' Hatton says: '. . . care should be taken not to assume too readily – as it seems to this writer that Fischer has done – that specific national objectives expressed during the war presuppose more than vague aspirations before August 1914.'[3]

Fischer and members of his school have done well to emphasize the need for deeper research into the social and economic background of the war and its causes. For Fischer the war represents a deep-rooted drive to turn Germany into a world power and, as James Joll says, he endeavours to show that 'there is more continuity between 1914 and 1933 or 1941 than many Germans would like to admit.' Certainly the First World War unleashed tremendous forces and in many respects set the pattern for the subsequent history of the twentieth century. In general, however, historians would be wise not to allow the course of events since 1914 to affect their treatment of the origins of the conflict.

Fischer and Geiss have paid inadequate attention to military and strategic problems. The crisis of 1914 cannot be understood without thorough knowledge of the balance of military power, the significance of the Schlieffen Plan, the implications of the Austrian Plan B and Plan R, and the problems associated with Russian mobilization. Fischer and Geiss treat these questions in a haphazard manner, and their lack of interest in military issues has led them into grave misinterpretations.

Imanuel Geiss says:

The outbreak of the First World War was not the result of blind, unfathomable fate, nor need its causes defy rational analysis by the historian.

[3] P. H. S. Hatton, 'Britain and Germany in 1914', *PP*, April 1967, pp. 138–43. See also J. Joll, *1914. The Unspoken Assumptions* (London, 1968), pp. 7–8.

There is no reason to refer the matter to some inscrutable higher force nor to give up in despair, in a fit of what has been called 'historical nihilism'.[4]

This is true, but 'rational analysis' indicates that the outbreak of war in 1914 was essentially a tragedy of miscalculation.

Looking back at the origins of the war as a whole, the story seems to be dominated by the consequences of 1870 and racial tensions in Eastern Europe. Granted wise leadership in Germany, these questions need not have exploded in a major conflict. Between 1890 and 1905 the deplorable naval policy of the Kaiser and the pressures exerted by the Pan-German League, the Navy League, and other nationalists did grave harm to Germany's reputation, but did not place her in direct peril. The miscalculations of Bülow and Holstein over Morocco led directly to the forming of the Triple Entente but for some years it was only a loose combination. Germany did not originate the Bosnian crisis, but Bülow's veiled ultimatum to Russia in March 1909 raised the prospect of a general war. However, Russia was in no condition to fight, and it seems that if Austria had followed up her surrender by attacking Serbia, then this outpost of Russian influence in the Balkans would have been eliminated. In that case the events of 1912–14 could not have occurred. From the aspect of *Realpolitik*, it would have been to Germany's advantage to exert more ruthless pressure on her ally in 1909.

In 1910–11 Germany had every reason to be cautious, but Kiderlen's bluster and Bethmann's inexperience lured her into the folly of Agadir. The consequences were momentous. Italy's attack on Turkey stirred the Balkan states, while France's national revival and the tightening of her defence bonds with Britain encouraged her to challenge Germany diplomatically and revived thoughts of military *revanche*. The unpredictable twists of Russian policy and the irresponsibility of her military chiefs aggravated the tensions and nearly led to the outbreak of the Great War in 1912. The events of 1912–13 saw the emergence of Poincaré, whose leadership contributed immeasurably to the revival of French power.

The outcome of the Balkan Wars posed a mortal threat to Austria–Hungary; Germany should never have allowed the Balkan states to attack Turkey; nor should she have tolerated the isolation and crushing of Bulgaria. From the autumn of 1913,

[4] Geiss, *July 1914*, p. 361.

German policy floundered without any clear purpose. The armaments race and the formidable development of Russian military power must soon have led to a major crisis although, if Europe had avoided disaster in July 1914, moderate and pacific forces might have asserted their ascendancy and arrested the headlong descent to war.

After Sarajevo, Wilhelm II and Bethmann Hollweg courted a great war and, in view of the prevailing mood in Paris and St. Petersburg, there was little hope of averting catastrophe after the Austrian ultimatum was presented in Belgrade. The crisis got out of control because Bethmann pushed Austria into a premature declaration of war on Serbia, while Paléologue and the French General Staff drove Russia along the fatal path to mobilization. The conduct of Paléologue and Joffre reflected French confidence in victory, but was also a reaction to the German war plan devised by Count von Schlieffen. That plan, with its flagrant violations of neutrality, had been approved by the German Government since 1904. In the final phase, military considerations were of decisive importance; they accelerated the whole tempo of events and confirmed the truth of Count Metternich's dictum: 'When the statesman has to yield to the soldier in peace or war, a people is usually doomed.'

Historians have been so absorbed in analysing 'the causes of the war' that they have neglected the strength of pacific sentiment in 1914. In Russia many conservatives agreed with Kokovtzov that war would unlock the flood gates of revolution; the majority of Frenchmen were pacific and Caillaux and Jaurès preached peace and conciliation; in Germany there was no irresistible drive to war and many economists and industrialists wanted peace; in Britain Grey would have had most liberals on his side when he declared that a great war would shatter the fabric of western civilization. Yet Churchill says:

... there was a strange temper in the air. Unsatisfied by material prosperity, the nations turned fiercely towards strife internal or external. National passions, unduly exalted in the decline of religion, burned beneath the surface of nearly every land with fierce, if shrouded, fires. Almost one might think the world wished to suffer. Certainly men were everywhere eager to dare.[5]

---

[5] Churchill, *The World Crisis 1911–1914*, p. 188.

Bibliographical Note

For books published before 1942, there is a good bibliography in L. Albertini, *The Origins of the War of 1914*. 3 vols. (London, 1952–7; 2nd ed., 1965). For detailed analysis of memoirs and documentary collections listed in Albertini see G. P. Gooch, *Recent Revelations of European Diplomacy* (London, 1940). There is a useful bibliographical note in A. J. P. Taylor, *The Struggle for Mastery in Europe 1848–1918* (Oxford, 1954). For books and articles published since 1942, there are substantial bibliographies in F. Fischer, *Germany's Aims in the First World War* (London, 1967) and I. Geiss, *July 1914* (London, 1967). J. A. Moses, *The War Aims of Imperial Germany: Professor Fritz Fischer and his Critics* (University of Queensland, 1968) is of outstanding importance.

Most of the significant documentary collections are listed in Albertini and analyzed by Gooch, although the Italian diplomatic documents were not published until the 1960s. I. Geiss, *Julikrise und Kriegsausbruch*, 2 vols. (Hannover, 1963–4) and his shorter *July 1914* are valuable collections but must be supplemented by reference to the numerous documents quoted by Albertini. However, the translations in Albertini must be treated with considerable caution.

Of the many books written before 1939, only two can be classified as histories of the first rank – S. B. Fay, *The Origins of the World War*, 2 vols. (New York, 1928) and B. E. Schmitt, *The Coming of the War*, 2 vols. (New York, 1930). They can still be consulted with profit, but were written before the publication of most of the Austrian, Russian and French documents.

Fay and Schmitt have been largely superseded by the great work of Albertini, published posthumously in Italian in 1942, and deservedly recognized as one of the finest achievements of modern scholarship. Albertini combines monumental research with a lucid and vigorous style and his phenomenal knowledge of the documents is illustrated on every page. He is tremendously strong on 1914 and very good on the Bosnian Crisis of 1908–9. His treatment of the Balkan Wars is less satisfactory and must be supplemented by E. C. Helmreich, *The Diplomacy of the Balkan Wars, 1912–1913* (Cambridge, Mass., 1938) and E. C. Thaden, *Russia and the Balkan Alliance of 1912* (University of Pennsylvania, 1965).

Albertini is weak on the Moroccan crises and the forming of the Triple Entente; on these questions see Taylor, *The Struggle for Mastery in Europe 1848–1918*, G. Monger, *The End of Isolation, British Foreign Policy 1900–1907* (London, 1963), N. Rich, *Friedrich von Holstein*, 2 vols. (Cambridge, 1965) and N. Rich and M. H. Fisher (eds.), *The Holstein Papers*, Vol. IV (Cambridge, 1963). A first-rate study of the Agadir crisis remains to be written. On the whole period, there is much solid information in G. P. Gooch, *Before the War, Studies in Diplomacy*, 2 vols. (London 1936–8).

Albertini discusses strategic questions with remarkable insight, but many of the key documents were not available to him. On military issues see the distinguished works of G. Ritter, *Staatskunst und Kriegshandwerk*, Vol. II (München, 1965) and *The Schlieffen Plan* (New York, 1958). Winston Churchill's brilliant but erratic *The World Crisis: The Eastern Front* (London, 1931) should also be consulted. A. J. P. Taylor's astonishing *tour de force*, *War by Time-Table* (London, 1969) is gravely misleading on the Schlieffen Plan of 1905 and ignores Moltke's vital modification of 1911. On naval affairs, A. J. Marder, *From the Dreadnought to Scapa Flow*, Vol. I (London, 1961) is a masterly study of the Royal Navy, but the German Navy still awaits a similar work. However, there is some material in Ritter's *Staatskunst*.

Schmitt wrote of Albertini: '. . . his work is strictly diplomatic history of the conventional type, that is, a record of the exchanges between governments. It does not discuss, except incidentally, the great disruptive tendencies of the age. . . .' When Fritz Fischer published his *Griff nach der Weltmacht* (Düsseldorf, 1961), he was making the first major attempt to approach the problem of war origins from a new angle. Michael Kitch says: '. . . the controversy generated by Fischer's work, which today overshadows the study of war origins and war aims, marks a decisive shift away from a strictly diplomatic approach to these problems to a more integrated one in which diplomacy is placed within a framework of political, social and economic forces.' Whatever may be thought of Fischer's handling of Imperial Germany, he has opened up a vast field of research which could be exploited to great advantage by British, French and Russian scholars.

On public opinion and newspaper comment, there are two illuminating books by E. M. Carroll, *Germany and the Great Powers, 1866–1914* (New York, 1938) and *French Public Opinion and Foreign Affairs, 1870–1914* (Harden, 1964). See also E. Weber, *The Nationalist Revival in France, 1905–1914* (Berkeley, 1959) and O. J. Hale, *Publicity and Diplomacy* (London, 1940).

On Eastern Europe see M. S. Anderson, *The Eastern Question 1774–1923* (London, 1966), A. J. May, *The Habsburg Monarchy, 1867–1914* (Cambridge, 1963), J. Remak, *Sarajevo* (London, 1959), and V. Dedijer, *The Road to Sarajevo* (London, 1967). In this category, W. S. Vucinich, *Serbia between East and West* (London, 1954) is in a class by itself, but unfortunately does not go beyond 1908.

Attempts to summarize the origins of the war in short concise books have not been very successful although P. Renouvin, *The Immediate Origins of the War* (London, 1928) was a brilliant effort in the light of the information available at the time. N. Mansergh, *The Coming of the First*

World War (London, 1949) is well written but badly outdated. D. E. Lee (ed.), *The Outbreak of The First World War: Who was responsible?* (New York, 1963) is clogged with out-of-date material. L. Lafore, *The Long Fuse* (London, 1966) makes interesting observations; although useful on Eastern Europe, it is marred by numerous errors and virtually ignores Agadir. J. Remak, *The Origins of World War I* (New York, 1967) has some penetrating comments on the deeper causes of the war, but is very thin on many major issues.

There is some very stimulating material in A. J. P. Taylor and J. M. Roberts (eds.), *History of the 20th Century* (London, 1968–9). The relevant chapters in the *New Cambridge Modern History Vol XII, The Shifting Balance of World Forces 1898–1945* (Cambridge, 1968) merit careful attention.

The subject has an irresistible attraction for amateur historians. G. M. Thomson, *The Twelve Days: 24 July to 4 August 1914* (London, 1964) is extremely interesting and conveys the tension and drama of the crisis. B. Tuchman, *The Proud Tower* (London, 1967) was an experiment which did not come off; her well-known *August 1914* (London, 1962) was said by Senator Robert Kennedy to have guided his brother during the Cuban crisis of 1962. This is a strange claim for a book which contains virtually no information on the outbreak of war.

Published works and articles used in the writing of this book are listed in the footnotes. To reduce the number of footnotes, references to documents have been omitted apart from unusual items of exceptional importance. By referring to date or time, the reader should have little difficulty in identifying a particular document and checking it in the appropriate collection.

Index